To Peter,

Jn 4:16

What Others are Saying About
Three Passions of the Soul

Bruce Terpstra serves up some real soul food in this book. It is seasoned with rich insights and observations from a lifetime of experience helping people become themselves. If you'd like to grow into your own skin, I recommend that you take big helpings of what he has to offer. Each chapter will prompt a soul-full conversation that will have you coming back for seconds.

Reggie McNeal,
best-selling author and leadership coach,
A Work of Heart: Understanding How God Shapes Spiritual Leaders
and *Practicing Greatness: Seven Disciplines of Extraordinary Spiritual Leaders*.

You know it's a good book when either you have to put the book down at times and step away, or you can't put the book down to step away for anything. This pendulum swing defined my reading of Bruce Terpstra's enlightening new book on faith formation, *Three Passions of the Soul*.

Leonard Sweet,
best-selling author (*Bad Habits of Jesus*),
professor (Drew University, George Fox University, Tabor College),
and founder of preachthestory.com.

The Gospel is simple but the transformation it brings goes to the deepest places of our soul. In *The Three Passions of the Soul*, Dr. Bruce Terpstra unpacks this miracle of soul transformation with a solid analysis of true discipleship. I have worked alongside Bruce for nearly 20 years. He lives what he writes. I have watched him faithfully lead people into the truth of these pages. This book is not just theory or empty theology. It works in real life with real people.

Dr. Ron Walborn,
Dean of Alliance Theological Seminary,
Nyack, New York.

In *Three Passions of the Soul*, Dr. Terpstra provides an insightful and meaningful contribution to the vital subject of discipleship. In my reading it, I was challenged to reflect upon my own spiritual development as well as what has been lacking in my investment in others.

Dr. John Stumbo,
President of the Christian and Missionary Alliance,
author of *An Honest Look at a Mysterious Journey*
and *In the Midst: Treasures from the Dark.*

Bruce is right: We must get at issues of our souls in disciple making. The *Three Passions of the Soul* effectively gives us a great tool to do so. Bruce's work as an overseer of pastors and churches over the years has given him a front row seat to how our core motivations (without a deep rooting in Christ) can badly damage ourselves and those around us. Offering us the gift of The Strength Deployment Inventory (SDI) as a core tool to help us get at our souls will be a gift for many pastors, leaders and churches in the years to come.

Pete Scazzero,
founding pastor of New Life Fellowship Church
and author of *The Emotionally Healthy Leader*
and *Emotionally Healthy Spirituality.*

This is an outstanding treatment of the topic of spiritual formation and the need to integrate a new approach into traditional discipleship. I firmly believe that every pastor should read and digest this work and prayerfully consider how to adjust the discipleship efforts in the local church because of it.

Pastor Tim Keller,
Senior Pastor of Carlisle Alliance Church,
Pennsylvania.

Peter Rendell
April 2017

THREE
PASSIONS
OF THE SOUL

Acceptance

Significance

Safety/Security

THREE PASSIONS OF THE SOUL

A DEEP AND TRANSFORMING REORIENTATION OF THE SOUL

BRUCE K. TERPSTRA

FOREWORD BY WARREN BIRD

Clovercroft Publishing

THREE PASSIONS OF THE SOUL

©2017 by Bruce K. Terpstra

Published by Clovercroft Publishing, Franklin, Tennessee

Published in association with Larry Carpenter of Christian Book Services, LLC

www.christianbookservices.com

Interior Design by Adept Content Solutions

Cover Design by Debbie Manning Sheppard

Illustrations by Timothy Mattson

Printed in the United States of America

978-1-942587-90-3

DEDICATION

I dedicate this book to my dad, who was an avid reader and wanted more than anything to read this book before he entered the presence of God. However, God took him home before it was completed. With his last breath, he told me that he loved me and was proud of me. Actually, those last words washed over me like an ocean wave that knocked me off my feet. As I was writing about soul discipleship and the connection to living in *sonship*, I personally had never heard my father say, "I love you." He may have said it. I never heard it.

Don't get me wrong, I knew his love. He was a gentleman who cared deeply for his family. Our greatest connections were on vacations where he disconnected himself from his work as a rocket scientist. His work focused on designing guidance systems which took men to the moon. Playing in the surf and camping in the outdoors are memories that I will treasure.

But hearing dad say "I love you" loosed something in my soul. Hearing him say "I am proud of you" touched something in me that I hadn't known before. Gasping for his last breath with failing lungs, these words made a difference in me. Hearing a father say that he loves you is transforming.

Thank you, Dad, for life, your love, and for the joy of hearing you say these words.

FOREWORD

This insightful book could be titled *Soul Discipleship* or *When Discipleship Transforms Your Soul*. If my soul is the place that drives my thoughts, emotions and behaviors, then discipleship must help me understand and deal with the formation of my soul.

That's the big idea behind this book as it advocates the kind of discipleship that goes far beyond treating merely the symptoms of my sin disease. True discipleship gets to the core of our being, especially the motivations that drive our pursuit of self-worth. It builds self-awareness of our motivations, allowing the love of God, through the deep work of the Holy Spirit, to transform us.

That message is much needed for today, especially in this era that looks for authenticity and honesty—hungering for it, and being drawn when finding it.

When Bruce Terpstra asked me to write this Foreword, he had no idea that the verse that becomes the metaphor for the entire book contain the very words that caused me as a teenager to give up on my own efforts and invite God to transform my soul. The book is rich with Scripture, but it starts with Jesus's words to the Pharisees in Matthew 23. Jesus likened their lives to a cup, and he points out how foolish and hypocritical it is for them to put so much effort into making the outside of the cup look good, but then doing nothing to treat the mess that's inside the cup.

That was the story of my life too as I focused on symptoms rather than root causes. If my soul is the place where I find meaning in life, the core of what I am and what I live for, then I needed a powerful work of God to clean me from the inside out. That decision to invite God to do whatever it takes to transform my inmost being is what started my journey of real discipleship, one that has led me ever deeper into the arms of a loving Heavenly Father, day after day and year after year.

Bruce weaves his own powerful story throughout the book, plus examples from others. His vulnerable narrative, his step-by-step development of his big idea, and his short chapters that end in excellent reflection questions all combine into a substantial foundation for how to approach the task of discipleship.

Three Passions of the Soul is full of treasures to nurture your own soul. Let it apply the truths of the gospel to your beneath-the-surface motivations. But let it also help you as you disciple others, shifting from emphasis on people's outward behaviors to what is in their hearts motivating those actions and attitudes.

May this book lead you to read the Bible with a new lens. May it lead you toward better answers for questions in the three areas Bruce zeroes in on: "am I accepted?" "am I significant?" and "am I safe?" Then may it lead you to disciple others with a depth that bears so much genuine life change that others are drawn to it, asking how they too can have a similar encounter with something divine.

Rev. Warren Bird, a long-time ministry co-laborer with Bruce Terpstra in the Metropolitan District C&MA, is the author or co-author of 31 books for ministry leaders, teaches at Alliance Theological Seminary, and serves as research director for Leadership Network.

CONTENTS

PREFACE

The discipline of writing necessarily brings clarity to the heart of the writer. For a long time, I have been processing both internally and externally with peers and pastors about growing convictions that have been gnawing at my soul. Writing these thoughts in an orderly way brings not only clarity of insight but also raises questions that have yet to be explored. It is my hope that growth will come to me the writer, through putting things in print. Putting new ideas in print is also a little scary. Making your thoughts public to the greater Christian community invites critical thinking of people of greater weight and stature. I welcome the dialogue that will ensue because of this kind of critique.

I am also writing because I desire to see the greater Christian church advance. If, in some small way, this effort can help others grow in their understanding of the soul and how the Gospel interacts with it, I will have achieved my purpose. To those in my tribe (denomination) whom I serve, I have a special burden to share these ideas in a way that can bring a positive change. It has been rich to have meaningful conversation about discipleship and the cleaning of the inside of the cup.

It is not my desire or purpose to prescribe a new program or tell anyone how to go about discipling the people entrusted to your care. I am not offering a "system of discipleship." Your own context, giftedness, culture, and personality will require different approaches. The diversity of God's community of faith will undoubtedly result in creative application of the truths contained in this book. I don't believe that God intended for us to do discipleship by way of a system or he would have revealed the system to us. I don't see systems or programs in the Bible. What we do have in the Scriptures are stories of God's pursuit of man's wayward soul. Each story gives us insight into our own soul. So if you are looking for a how-to-book, you will be disappointed. But if you are looking for some deeper thought into the soul and how the Gospel impacts the soul, I believe you will find treasure that will nurture your journey with God.

In the following pages, I will touch on different approaches of discipleship that have been practiced by godly men and women throughout the ages. It is not my intent to stomp my feet on anyone, let alone any individual. But I do feel it necessary to draw some distinctions from what I am calling the "soul discipleship." To draw some comparisons and distinctions, I necessarily must make generalizations of which many may be unfair to someone in particular. The truth is I personally have had some experience in each of these discipleship focuses. I have sat under some of these approaches as a student and others I have led as pastor. All of these have contributed to my growth and maturity (as well as my sin, pride, blindness, superficiality, and pharisaical behavior).

My shelf is full of books on discipleship, so why write another one? It seems like a new book on this topic, and others like it (spiritual formation, spiritual direction, coaching, etc.) is being printed daily. The number of books on the market today demonstrates two things to me. Clearly, there is dissatisfaction with what is happening in the church regarding discipleship. I don't think there is any question about it. There is a hunger and thirst for something that will bring life to our faith. There is something lacking.

Additionally, I believe God is stirring the church worldwide with greater passion for a deeper discipleship. Books like *Radical* by David Platt and *Not a Fan* by Kyle Idleman have demonstrated that there is a thirst for God that is like a deer panting for water. Both books call for a greater commitment to Christ and have become very popular (at least for the moment). It is not my purpose to advocate these books or their theology, but they do demonstrate dissatisfaction with the state of discipleship in the church today. And there seems to be agreement on this truth. How to get there and where we are going is another matter.

When I read a book, I like to know the background of the writer. It helps me to understand their influences and perspectives. I was raised by Christian parents in an Independent Fundamentalist Church that was struggling to break out of its fundamentalist roots. For example, my pastor, growing up, took a vacation and came back with a beard. His job was threatened so he shaved the beard. You get the idea. It was a growing church in the suburb of

Metro New York. People were regularly baptized and Sunday school on steroids was the discipleship approach. My love for God's Word was developed during these formative years. It was here that I was baptized in my teens as my faith became my own. It was ingrained in me early to distrust denominational Christianity, especially Catholicism. By God's grace, I was led by the Spirit to discover people who were disciples of Jesus from other stripes.

My journey led me to serve in the following denominations for different lengths of time: Evangelical Lutheran, American Baptist, United Methodist/ Presbyterian USA, and Christian and Missionary Alliance. I have degrees in psychology, theology, and leadership. I love to read, especially from different thought leaders other than my own tribe. Perhaps this eclectic background has made me most comfortable in my tribe of the Christian and Missionary Alliance for the past twenty-six years. Ultimately, we are people of the book. Christ is central. The Gospel is our message. Our mission is to bring the message of Christ to the world.

Before taking the journey into the soul, I want to acknowledge a few people who have shaped my own soul. There are many so I can't mention them all. My mentor of twenty-five years, John Soper, has taught me to lead with humility. Richard Bush has been a deep thinker and a help in probing my own soul. John Owen, even though I have never met the man (I'm not that old!), has shaped my appreciation for my own sinful nature and the great grace of God. I have read more books from one writer who has impacted me from a distance in the past thirty-five years, and more recently through personal teaching and interaction, Larry Crabb. I am grateful for the influence of these men in my life. I apologize in advance for thoughts claimed as my own, which were germinated by these men or directly quoted, but have failed to remember the origin of my thoughts.

The staff of the Metropolitan District of the Christian and Missionary Alliance (Doug Bortner, Paul Keidel, Yeathus Johnson, David Janssen, and Bob Riconda), as well as a group of prominent pastors in the New York area, have travelled the journey of writing this book with me. Their insights and fingerprints are all over the manuscript as we wrestled together with what it means to disciple more deeply. Thank you for your partnership in ministry.

Burning Question: Am I Missing Something?

I felt my face rush with blood as I blushed from inner fear and panic about my own soul. I was in an eight-month training program to become a more effective leader and was being instructed about how different people are motivated. I was awakened to the reality of my soul—the inner man. I came under strong conviction by the conviction of the Spirit about what was driving much of my own behavior and ministry. This awakening began a journey of discovery and reading the Bible with a new lens that I didn't have before. It would change the way I would understand the Gospel and the nature of discipleship.

I am embarrassed (but probably not alone) in delving into the subject of discipleship deeply for the first time in my thirty-five years of public ministry. Yes! This is true! It is hard to believe that discipleship has been a back-burner issue for me for so long. Ironically, I was sold out to completing the great commission: "Go and make disciples of all nations, baptizing them in the name of the Father, Son, and Holy Spirit, teaching them to obey all my commands." I memorized that Scripture and required others to do likewise. I even believed I was pretty effective at doing the great commission. I received awards from my denomination for leading the way in church planting. I taught hundreds of people to effectively share the Gospel. My ministry experienced significant growth and baptisms year after year. I never compromised in teaching to be appealing or attract not-yet believers. I taught my disciples to obey everything that Jesus taught. But if I am honest with myself, there was always a nagging feeling that something was not right.

I was focused on catching the fish, not cleaning it. Cleaning fish is smelly. Actually, it stinks. It is best left to others. Earlier on in my ministry, I was pursuing a master's degree in Christian counseling. I found it tedious and mind numbing. Who wants to listen to other people's problems all day long and then have them repeat the same story with different actors or circumstances over and over again without seeing significant change. I opted for preaching and teaching "the Gospel." In my limited experience, I believed people had been changed (at least on the outside and for a time). I knew the fish had to be cleaned, so I devised different ways of getting this done. Primary to my approach was the systematic and exegetical approach to preaching the Word of God.

Recently, my wife suggested (demanded) that I finally sort through thirty-five years of sermons, and teaching notes and decide what I wanted to keep. As I started to read through them, beginning with the oldest, I was repulsed by what I saw and fired up the outside pizza oven (585 degrees burns poor sermons pretty quickly!). My wife appeared to the smell of burnt paper and ran into the backyard to rescue my life's work, risking chard limbs and singed nostrils! She was somewhat successful, but many words had already floated to the heavens as a holy sacrifice. Over the next several months, she began reading me some of my old sermons. They actually were pretty good if I don't say myself! Surely, they changed lives. And I am sure they did. God takes that which we offer him and uses it for his glory. His Word doesn't return void. But I have been in ministry too long to believe the lie that preaching alone will produce disciples.

Another device I used was the *Plant a Seed* booklet by Dr. James Kennedy (and others just like it).[1] This first-steps booklet taught new disciples the basic disciplines of reading the Bible, prayer, confession, worship, evangelism, and of course, tithing. It was kind of a starter kit for new believers. It was good to get them to start growing. Baby food and milk for the newborn was my thinking. I was satisfied that we were doing something to help the new disciples grow, however, after five weeks of training, there needed to be more.

My approach was to put them into small groups, which were remarkably successful. By successful, I mean that they attended regularly and felt loved and cared for. Who wouldn't be happy with eighty percent of your congregation being in a small group? Well, I was for a while. However, I didn't see much progress in what I deemed at the time to be what disciples should be doing. I even changed the group structure to process my sermons more deeply by providing the groups with "insightful" questions to apply what they were learning! My focus was on questions that would apply the Gospel to their lives so they would practice what they were learning. I wanted doers, not mere hearers, of the Word.

Another approach I took was to begin the Christian Life Institute. There was a questionnaire that was filled out upon application, and you had a curriculum of forty-eight classes that you could register, much like a college curriculum, according to your needs and deficiencies. There was great excitement for this developmental system, which included not only classes and teaching, but also internships and mentoring. However, it didn't accomplish what I had hoped for. Many people gained knowledge but failed to change. They still struggled with essentially the same issues. It seemed like the church was like a train that we (myself and my pastoral and elder team) were pushing up a steep hill.

My story is not unlike many other stories that I have heard from pastors and leaders. As a district overseer with almost four hundred pastors under my care, I can say with some degree of certainty that this is the story of most, if not all, of those who are called as undershepherds for the Great Shepherd.

I don't know if you ever have asked this question with regards to ministry: "Am I missing something?" Either there is something desperately wrong with the way I am doing ministry, or there is something desperately wrong with the Gospel because my vision for the church just isn't happening. For those of you who are golfers, it is like trying to hit the ball straight down the fairway, and you keep slicing to the right. No matter how much you try or how many adjustments you make in your swing, the ball keeps spinning

> *Either there is something desperately wrong with the way I am doing ministry, or there is something desperately wrong with the gospel.*

sideways, sometimes getting worse with more effort and practice. It can be very frustrating. Is it even possible to hit a golf ball straight and long? There is hope because occasionally it happens, and when it does, it is a beautiful thing.

xxii   Three Passions of the Soul

Reflection Questions

1. Are you satisfied with the results of discipleship that is happening in your church? Explain.

2. What is your vision for discipleship? In other words, what do you hope discipleship will produce in the lives of people?

3. The author is suggesting that we might be missing something in our approach to discipleship. What approaches to discipleship are you currently counting on to change lives?

4. How satisfied are you with your church's approach and success in making disciples that make disciples? Give reasons for your answer.

5. Ask God to give you an open heart to respond to the Spirit's guidance as you process discipleship through the tool of this book.

PART I

The Orientation of the Soul

*The heart is deceitful above all things, and
desperately sick; who can understand it?*

—Jeremiah 16:9

1

What Is in the Cup?

Woe to you, scribes and Pharisees, hypocrites! For you clean the
outside of the cup and the plate, but inside they are full of greed
and self-indulgence. You blind Pharisee! First clean the inside
of the cup and the plate, that the outside also may be clean.

—Matthew 23:25–26

There are a series of verses that I read rapidly and rarely pause because I don't see myself in them. In a rather long section in Matthew 23 where Jesus is condemning the Pharisees, he strongly condemns their work. Surely, this doesn't apply to me! To sum up the context of what Jesus is saying, he is condemning the *way* the Pharisees conduct their ministry. He sees them as the problem. He calls them "blind guides" (verse 16), among other names. But upon further inspection, there is a paragraph in that passage that now catches my attention. He says, "Woe to you, scribes and Pharisees, hypocrites! For you clean the outside of the cup and the plate, but inside they are full of greed and self-indulgence. You blind Pharisee! First

> *If you listen to many*
> *sermons that are*
> *preached, many of them*
> *are about cleaning up*
> *the outside of the cup.*

clean the inside of the cup and the plate, that the outside also may be clean"
(Matt. 23:25–26).

Don't miss this important truth. Jesus is certainly concerned about hypocrisy and condemns it. Ministry with hypocrisy is like the blind guide who
doesn't know where he himself is going. He is going to lead others into a ditch
or off a cliff. But there is a deeper truth here. The Pharisees were concerned
primarily with the outside of the cup. Their discipleship was about producing behavior that was in accordance with the revealed Scripture. But they
neglected the cleaning of the inside of the cup! This is the part of the cup or
bowl that can't be seen. It is the soul. It is the inner man. It is the motivation
of the heart. Jesus is getting to the center of discipleship, and it resembles
nothing of the ministry of the teachers of the law or the Pharisees (who were
people committed to holiness, or at least the display of holiness). Discipleship
has everything to do with the cleaning of the inner man—the soul.

If our discipleship is focused on outward behaviors that conform to Scriptural standards, we are doomed to failure. Jesus gives us great insight into how
disciples change. They must first change inside. You have to delve into the
recesses of the heart and discover what is driving the behavior. What is the
motivation? It is possible to do all the right things for none of the right reasons. If we keep cleaning the outside of the cup, we will never get anywhere.
We are destined to disappointment. We will be greatly disillusioned.

Woe to us if we don't change the focus of our discipleship. Getting more
people out for service projects will not achieve God's purposes. Learning
more Scripture and holding people accountable to biblical standards is more
akin to being a Pharisee than being a Christian. Getting people to a higher
percentage of worship services will not do the trick. Holding people accountable to greater obedience to expectations will surely fail.

And yes! We are missing something! We are missing the focus of applying
the truth of the Gospel to the soul. This book is about just that. It is about
discovering the power of the Gospel as it relates to the soul. This is the promise of Jesus. The inside of the cup is cleaned by the Gospel. Did you hear that?
Can that be true? Have we been trying to clean the outside of the cup? Have
we wasted all that energy even though we may have had wonderful motives?
I believe that much of our teaching and discipleship are closely related to
this fatal mistake. Few sermons are designed to understand the complexity
of the soul and what is driving behavior that is so out of line with godliness
and holiness.

In this book, I will explore the soul and its motivations. The more we understand the soul and the motivations that drive it, the greater opportunity
we have to apply the glorious Gospel of Jesus Christ. In my faith journey, I

feel that I am just becoming awakened to my soul. I am growing in my understanding of the Gospel, and I am learning how to feast on its implications.

The truth is that I am a pretty nice guy. Most people would describe me as not only nice but kind, caring, and supportive. However, that description is only my persona (the outside of the cup). I have learned to keep the outside of my cup clean. If I didn't, I would lose my job! But who knows what the inside of the cup looks like? Who really know me? Regardless of whether you know the inside of my cup, that is the part that drives everything in my life. What if the motivation of my soul is to have you think highly of me so I "act" nice to you? Is that a righteous soul? Thirty-five years of ministry has taught me that some people are very good at cleaning the outside of the cup, but the inside is a mess. It is true of pastors as well. It is also true of me. It is why I need the Gospel for my soul. I am desperate for Christ to change my soul. And Christ is all-powerful and able to do that deep work.

As a district superintendent who gives oversight to many pastors and is also responsible to the churches they serve, I can tell you that what is on the outside of the cup doesn't always reflect what is on the inside. When things get difficult in the church, the inside of the cup gets revealed. After all these years, I am still astonished at the filth on the inside of the cup. This is true not only of church members but of pastors. Bible college and seminary did not clean the inside of the cup. Years of ordination training did not do the job. Reading many books failed. Completing study guides with fill in the blanks apparently didn't make a great difference. Hate is spewed. Anger and wrath is flung with furry. Self-righteous positioning is set up like a brick wall that can't be penetrated with the most powerful Gospel truths that can be lobbed into the fray.

> *Our soul is the place where we find meaning, purpose. It is the place of identity.*

When the pressure is on, what is on the inside tends to get revealed. We can manage our life pretty well when everything is going well. But when life becomes uncontrollable, the real you pours out and soaks everyone. "Forgiveness" of past wrongs is forgotten in the battle. The bent bow of past pain is drawn back to powerfully and swiftly send arrows intended to defend our souls and attack those who threaten our life and expose who we really are in the soul. There is a sense of desperateness in all of this. It is as if our lives will not survive the onslaught. Our soul is in danger. Our soul is the place where we find meaning, purpose. It is the place of identity. It is the core of what we are and what we live for. It is the center of our most tightly held beliefs from which our intentions and behaviors are drawn.

My wife and I have been married for thirty-six years. Most of that time, we have been in full-time ministry (some joke that "full-time" means pastors are paid to be good, and everyone else is good for nothing). The outside of our cup looks pretty good. Being disciples of Jesus for a long time, we have grown year after year. We can point out milestones of our growth and faith in Christ. Almost all of them have a story of pain attached to them. That is often when the inside of the cup gets revealed.

One day, a county sheriff came to our door. That is never a good thing, especially if you are a district superintendent. I have been sued eight times. The notice of lawsuit comes in a registered letter or is hand delivered by a sheriff. This notice, however, was different. It was delivered to my wife! She was in shock. Now if you knew my wife, you would know that this would be a life-changing experience. Of course, I was completely calm. Well, at least on the outside.

With many tears in her eyes, she; read the lawsuit repeatedly, digesting the threatening situation and the ramifications for our family. She didn't recognize the name of the person or the incident, but she was being named as someone who assisted a man in stealing a large amount of money from his parents. You see, my wife is a paralegal in a law office. She is also a notary. After much searching of her memory and replaying an incident over and over in her mind, she came to the conclusion that she had notarized a document for a man who had fraudulently used the document to steal money. She found his name and a copy of his driver's license in her notary book, so she did everything correctly, but this did not alleviate the intense anxiety and fear she was experiencing. We will never know what happened because we were told the man who stole the money spent it all and then took his own life. The lawsuit was being filed by his own parents whom he stole the money.

> It was in the midst of this storm that God spoke to us.

Guilt flooded my wife's soul. She struggled to sleep at night as she worried that she had done something that possibly cost someone their life's savings. And potentially, her actions could take everything we have as well. This anxiety grew until she started having panic attacks for the first time in her life. As a husband, it was painful to watch her struggle. We read Scriptures, we prayed, but the anxiety grew. I too found myself descending into the cavern of anxiety and found it difficult to sleep. It was during this time that we discovered that there was no insurance to cover her actions. These were very dark and lonely days.

In despair, we cried out to God, "Why would you allow such injustice? After all these years of serving you, it isn't right that you would take everything away. How will I provide for our family as we enter the retirement years and our health begins to fail (the latter was already happening)?" These and other questions weighed heavily. Where was the rescue, like the disciples had on the Sea of Galilee during the great storm?

It came in the form of a question: "Why were you okay when I took away everything from you when you planted a church in Wayne, New Jersey? But now, when you are being threatened, you are failing in your faith?" You see, when we had planted a church in Wayne, we bought a house before we had sold our old home. After two years, hardly anyone had looked at it. Even by trying to sell it at an extreme loss (housing market had tanked), no offers came. No one even looked at it. Eventually, we lost the home we had agreed to purchase and our ten percent deposit on our new home. Then we sold the old home at a loss and had nothing to our name. But we kept our eyes on Jesus, believing that God was in the plan. Or better yet, we were in God's plan. Why was this time so different from the first time we lost everything? What happened to us?

This started us on a journey of seeing how we had transferred our security from God to our money. To put it another way, our savings became our idol. We loved our money more than God. That may sound harsh, but it was true. The more quickly we repented of this reality, we knew we would be restored to peace. That is exactly what we did. We did it out loud on our bed, agreeing with God about our sin. There was an immediate peace that came over us. The lawsuit was still there. Our lives were still being threatened, but our security had shifted. God was our security once again. Nothing could shake that. Nothing.

It would take another year to sort out the lawsuit. God never deserted us. In the end, the law office insurance agreed to cover my wife. There was a settlement that cost us a little. Later, we were told that the document my wife notarized was never even used to steal the money. Because the settlement agreement was confidential, I can't share the details of what really happened, but I can tell

> *What I have discovered is that there are three primary motivators of the soul. Ignatius of Loyola, all the way back in the fifteenth century, called them the "passions of the soul."*

you my wife had nothing to do with what happened in this case at all. What a damaged, messed-up world we live in! But, today, I am thankful that we went through the experience. It shifted our focus. I learned that discipleship is a lifetime journey. It is not static, nor is it always on an incline upward.

By the way, there are hundreds of stories like that one (maybe not as dramatic) that I can recall. It occurs to me that God is so gracious and patient with us on this journey. The stories of brokenness are also stories of God's mercy and grace. His love abounds to his children. This is important as we examine the task of discipleship. Any approach to discipleship that does not reflect the heart and grace of the Father is not Christian discipleship. God's heart is enduring, patient, and long-suffering. He doesn't give up on us and is slow to anger.

The soul. How is your soul? Is it being transformed by the Gospel? In what ways? What is driving your behavior? Are you aware of what is beneath the surface and driving what you do? What if you were to become aware of what is driving your own behavior? The desert fathers in the third century identified three motivators as well that tie into these same powers. The mystics of the fifteenth century also wrote about these passions of the soul, which they called, "inordinate attachments." Jesus himself alluded to them when he was discipling the rich man. This book will seek to unpack the passions of the soul and how they related to discipleship.

Here is the central point of this book. God (Father, Son, and Holy Spirit) created us in his image. The nature of that image is relational. We were created as image-bearers to give glory to God. God is love. Our soul was designed to receive the love of God and live a life of love toward others. There are three passions of the soul: acceptance, significance, and security. We are always asking the questions: (1) Am I accepted? (2) Am I significant? and (3) Am I safe? These three passions of the soul are descriptors of how we receive and give love. Apart from the Gospel and the regeneration of our soul, we are driven along in life to meet these innate needs apart from God without satisfaction. This leads us into a life of sin and desperation. We fail to love as God loves. We use others to fill the void left by the Fall. In God's mercy, he awakens us to his divine love and grace through the Gospel. The task of discipleship is the formation of the soul to know this divine love and live a life of love toward others. Discipleship is futile apart from discipleship of the soul, also called the heart. (The terms *soul* and *heart* are used in many ways, but very often, they describe the motivation of our being.) By growing in the Holy Spirit, awareness of the soul's passion and how we seek love apart from God, we have the opportunity to confess and repent. We have the opening to find our identity in God's love. True freedom in Christ is released as we live in the lavish love of God. This love is revealed to us by Jesus Christ, the exact representation of the Father.

This book will systematically work through these truths—unpacking the Scriptures. The first section of the book lays the foundational goal of discipleship. The second section will address the anatomy of the soul and its implications to discipleship. The third section will lay out a vision for soul discipleship based on the three passions of the soul. May the Lord speak to you through his Spirit, as you reflect on the words of this book and ponder the lavish love of God.

In an effort to walk through these life-changing truths in a way that integrates the fullness of Scripture, I have developed a graphic that should help us. The graphic will begin simply but will be built out in more complexity as we travel through the Scripture together.

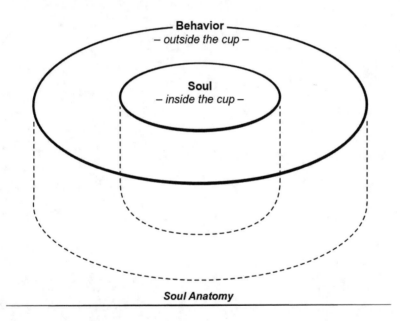

Soul Anatomy

The soul is the inside of the cup. This is the place that discipleship must address. On the outside, we have the visual behaviors of a person. Most discipleship addresses this "outer cup" aspect of a person's life. It is not an effective form of discipleship. There is also a shell that surrounds the soul. This shell is not to be mistaken as the soul. It is both the filter for how the soul perceives itself as well as the barrier that keeps the soul from being addressed. The Scripture uses the word *flesh* to describe the shell. It shapes the soul in ways that are at antithesis with Christ.

It is critical that we come to be familiar with what I am calling the "anat-omy of the soul." This simple diagram will help us to differentiate the many approaches to discipleship that fail to address the inside of the cup that Jesus speaks. It will also assist us in systematically unpacking the Scriptural teach-ing about the soul. Each chapter will contribute a greater understanding of this diagram and add pieces to it so that in the end you will have a model for soul discipleship that will be repeatable.

Before we begin to unpack the diagram of the anatomy of the soul, we must be clear about the goal of discipleship. If our goal is fuzzy, we will wander in our approach. Fortunately, the Scriptures are absolutely clear on this point. But for many, it is a mystery. If you understand the purpose of discipleship, you will take a very different approach to discipleship than you have in the past.

Reflection Questions

1. Think more deeply about what Jesus meant by "outside of the cup" discipleship versus "inside of the cup." What are some things the church does that is more like discipling outside of the cup?

2. Inside of the cup discipleship focuses on the soul and the motivation of the heart. Why is the motivation of the heart critical to discipleship?

3. Reflect on the three questions that people are asking and drive behavior. Am I accepted? Am I significant? Am I safe? Can you identify how these motivations drive your behavior? Give examples.

4. We all have stories of how God shaped us by his Gospel. The author told a personal story of a shaping story. Can you identify a shaping story and how the passions of the soul were at work in you (acceptance, significance, security)?

2

What Is the Goal of Discipleship?

> My little children, for whom I am again in the anguish
> of childbirth until Christ is formed in you!

—Galatians 4:19

At first glance, the question, "What is the goal of discipleship?" seems to be a no-brainer. The goal is clearly to become like Christ. The apostle Paul when writing to the churches in Galatia wrote, "My dear children, for whom I am again in the pains of childbirth until Christ is formed in you..." (Gal 4:19). The allusion to childbirth certainly indicates a process that is painful and doesn't come easy. Paul was struggling with the lack of progress of the Galatian believers. He says he is "perplexed" (Gal 4:20). He even is concerned that his discipling of the people in Galatia has not been in vain (Gal 2:2). How many of us have had that thought? For Paul, the goal is clear, but the process of formation is frustrating and perplexing.

The letter to the Galatians as a whole gives us some clue as to what Paul was frustrated about in regards to their formation. He discovered that the churches had deserted the Gospel that they had been taught and were teaching another gospel which was no gospel at all! (Gal 1:6–9). Even Peter had joined in this error. When we read more closely, we discover that the reason

13

this false gospel had developed legs was because people wanted to have the approval of others (Gal 1:10). People-pleasing was a problem. Already we have identified two issues of being like Christ: correct teaching about the Gospel and not being a people-pleaser. But there is more—much more. It is in the *much more* that the goal of discipleship becomes fuzzy and even misdirected.

This idea of being like Christ is vast and complex. Paul goes on to bring correction to the Galatians. Some additional issues he raises are how relationships between race, gender, class have been transformed; our unity in the midst of diversity; our adaption as sons of God; our inheritance that is guaranteed; what days to celebrate; the failure of the disciples to respect Paul; how to apply the Law; living in freedom; the coming hope and the Spirit of God and how this applies to how we live; how to run the race of life successfully, serve one another in love, love your neighbor as yourself, don't devour each other, walk in the Spirit, avoid the acts of the flesh, crucify the flesh with its passions and desires; don't be conceited or envy each other; restore sinners gently; watch out for temptation; carry each other's burdens; work hard and carry your own load; share with your instructor (pay the pastor) that a man reaps what he sows does it in the Spirit; do good and don't give up; care for the people of the church; and boast in the cross. And that is not a complete list! And this is just six chapters of one epistle!

> *What if the task that Jesus gave to us in making disciples had a narrower focus?*

Now when we go about the goal of making disciples who are like Christ, where will you focus? Some camp on the Gospel. If you understand the Gospel, then everything else will take care of itself. Others focus on justice issues: serving others, race relations, and gender equality. Others ruminate on theology because correct theology will address all the other issues. The theory is if you have correct theology, you will live righteously. Still others will focus on the character that the Spirit of God produces. The goal is Christian character. There are even others who will focus and zoom in on avoidance of the acts of the flesh. Others choose to emphasize the importance of crucifying the flesh as the key to discipleship. As you read these approaches to discipleship, you may have had specific people, churches, and denominations in mind. My purpose in this exercise is simply to illustrate that the goal of discipleship is both clear and very complicated. Paul was clear when he declared in Romans 8:29, "For those God foreknew he also predestined to be conformed to the image of his Son…" The confusion comes in when the scope of transformation is so wide and deep, we have no choice but to pick and choose what to focus on and emphasize. Later on in this book, we will examine common approaches to discipleship and how they are inadequate to produce Christlikeness.

Is there a simpler approach? I would suggest to you that we may be making discipling more complicated than it is. If we could address the issues of the heart that direct human behavior, we could focus on those and be more productive. When we take a step back and read the Bible as a complete story, our focus on what is critical begins to emerge. It is like the 3-D picture that looks flat and makes little sense until you stare at it long enough. Suddenly the picture pops! When you see it, you wonder why nobody else sees it. They too must go through the process of staring and focusing on the picture until it pops for them. My prayer is that the key to discipleship will pop for you as you read this book.

Reflection Questions

1. How has your goal of discipleship shaped your discipleship process?

2. Is your discipleship approach simple or complex? Explain.

3. Reflect on the teachings of Jesus and the apostles and what they are focused on in disciple-making. How is our approach similar or different from their focus?

3

What Does Love Have to Do With It?

If I speak in the tongues of men and of angels, but have not love,
I am a noisy gong or a clanging cymbal. And if I have prophetic
powers, and understand all mysteries and all knowledge, and
if I have all faith, so as to remove mountains, but have not
love, I am nothing. If I give away all I have, and if I deliver
up my body to be burned, but have not love, I gain nothing.

—1 Corinthians 13:1–3

C. S. Lewis once said, "A story is precisely the sort of thing that cannot be understood till you have heard the whole of it."[2] Have you ever asked the question, "What is the whole story of the Bible?" Perhaps by grasping the overall story of God, we might gain insight into what God is doing and his purposes. It is too easy to get swallowed up in one part of the story. Partial understanding or focus will lead us on the wrong path. I will attempt to make the case that the story of God is a love story. From beginning to end, the story of God is one of relationship—relationship that is pure, then broken, and then reconciled. This metanarrative drives everything else in the story.

The story begins with the Triune God. In Genesis 1, we read about the creation of the universe. In the first twenty-five verses, we read about the formation of the world as we know it, with all of its beauty and wonder. The Scripture says six times, "And God said, 'Let the...'." But there is an abrupt shift in the pattern beginning in verse 26 when God creates mankind. Here the text says, "Then God said, 'Let *us* make mankind in our image.'" The grammar clearly shifts to indicate that God (Elohim) as a Trinitarian community is creating mankind. From Genesis, we are not aware of the members of the Trinity, but we learn of the Father, Son, and the Holy Spirit later on in God's revelation. But right here in the beginning, we have the Trinity deciding together to create a being that is unique from the rest of creation.

> *...the story of God is a love story. From beginning to the end, the story of God is one of relationship—relationship that is pure, then broken, and then reconciled.*

We don't have the dialogue of the Trinity in any detail, but clearly, the members of the Trinity are conversing with one another and deciding about the nature of mankind. The Trinity is relating together and enjoying the process of creating. They are in perfect harmony and unity as they choose. Don't miss the truth that God is relational with the capacity to relate. To interact. To love.

The triune God decides that this unique creation of mankind will be different from all the other things and creatures. They decide to make mankind in "our image" and "our likeness." Man is created differently from the animals in that God breathes life into him, signifying an intimate relationship. Volumes have been written on the understanding of the image of God in man. Much of the discussion is speculation as there is not much information given in the text. The most popular ideas speculate that man is like God in the sense that he has personhood. Unique to personhood, it is understood that man has volition—he is able to choose. Others have suggested that man is unique in that he has a soul. This is the part of man that is able to reflect or have self-consciousness and is lasting. It focuses on the truth that man can relate to God.

Although it is interesting to speculate about the image of God in man, we are best served by the context in discovering what the significance of this "our likeness" is about. I would suggest to you that the context is about relationship. The change from the singular pronoun to that of the plural pronoun is a clue. The triune God is discussing amongst itself the creation of a being that is like them—relational. In other words, "Let us make a being that is like us in that we can have relationship with him like we have relationship together." The Godhead is in perfect unity and harmony together. There are no disagreements. We could describe this Trinitarian relationship as one of love. It is a pure and holy relationship. The Godhead is creating beings with this same capacity. Dr. Martin Lloyd Jones concludes that there is a twin relationship between the love of God and the goodness of God.[3] It is interesting that after the Trinity creates man, they declared, "It was very good." This relationship between man and God in all of its goodness is what God had in mind when the world was created. As Adam and Eve enjoyed the garden that God had created for them, they enjoyed the fellowship of the Godhead. In the cool of the day, God would visit with them (Gen 3:8). This is why he was created. He wanted to relate to his creation.

When man was created, he was made in the image of God and enjoyed a good and loving relationship with his creator. He reflected the glory of the Godhead in perfect love. It is important that we grasp the intent of God in this relationship as it is crucial to the story of God. God created man to be like himself in pure love and relationship with one another and with himself. I am making a case that love from the outset was that which characterized the relationship with the Trinity. It is not the only attribute, but the central attribute, in the story of man's creation. As central to the story of creation, it is sure to be central to the story of discipleship.

Before we move on, I want to take a detour and discuss for a moment other attributes of God and how they relate to love. I have moderated many oral ordination exams for pastors, and there is always an interesting discussion when discussing the attributes of God. A common question raised by the interviewer is, "What is the attribute of God that is supreme amongst all the others?" After some pause, the ordinand either chooses the holiness of God or the love of God. The argument for the holiness of God usually states that all the other attributes of God come from the holiness of God. Some ordinands incorrectly speak of the holiness of God as the righteousness of God. It is true that righteousness is part of God's holiness, but the idea of holiness is the idea of the separateness of God. He is not like any other. For example, because God is holy, he is not only righteous, but he is pure. His love is perfect. It lacks nothing.

Those who chose to emphasize the love of God as the supreme attribute of God point to the teachings of John, who declared, "God is love." It is his love that makes him separate from everything and everyone else. Obedience is always the result of love. John says, "And this is his command: to believe in the name of his Son, Jesus Christ, and to love one another as he commanded us. The one who keeps God's commands lives in him" (1 John 3:23–24). This is the teaching of the apostle John over and over again. Obedience is the result of love. John 15:9–10 says, "As the Father has loved me, so have I loved you. Now remain in my love. If you keep my commands, you will remain in my love, just as I have kept my Father's commands and remain in his love."

Dr. Martin Lloyd Jones discusses the relationship between the primary attributes of God: "You notice the order in which we are taking them—holiness, righteousness and justice, goodness and love. It is a dangerous and terrible thing not to put these attributes in the right order. People have often been guilty of that, and the result is that they have made shipwreck of their faith.[4] I am not taking issue with Dr. Jones's analysis. He may very well be right. However, I am not as sure as he is that you can divide these characteristics. He himself says that love and goodness are so closely related that you can't really divide them. The same can be said of holiness and righteousness or holiness and love.

What I would argue for is a holy love. Not a love that is unholy. But rather, a love that is pure. Love can be corrupted. And it has been. We all have stories to tell about how we have been injured by impure love. But God's love is pure and holy and good. There is perfect love within the Trinity—Father, Son, and Spirit. And there was perfect love in the garden at the start of Creation between the Trinity and man. I would even argue that this is what was lost in the Fall. It was the break in relationship that was so tragic.

There are those who would focus more on the holiness of God, and that the story of the Fall was more about the breaking of God's law. Man disobeyed God and ate the fruit of the forbidden tree. If you make the holiness of God and righteousness the focus of the story, your discipleship will naturally become about living righteously. It will be about law keeping and avoiding sin. Your goal will be right living or moral living. The Gospel then is a gospel of living rightly because Jesus paid for our sin. It is a legal transaction. If you listen to the presentation of the Gospel by many people, that is the focus of the story. They make it a law story. The story of God's love and our being created in the image of God to be image bearers of that love like God only briefly makes it into the story, when John 3:16 is quoted, "For God so loved the world…" But isn't the whole story about love? Wasn't both creation and reconciliation motivated by God's pure and holy love?

I was speaking to just such a person who will remain unnamed. He couldn't buy into the idea that love was central to the story of God. He chose holiness over love. As I expressed my approach to discipleship that focused on a loving

God who created a world where the glory of his love would be reflected in his creation, and how love is the goal of discipleship, he objected with vigor. He believed that obedience was the goal because we are to be "holy because God is holy" (1 Pet 16). Peter goes on to say that without holiness, no one will see God. Living righteously was clearly his goal and focus.

> *This is love: that God sent his Son into the world to atone for our sins.*

If you read the context of 1 Peter 1, you will discover that Peter himself was closer to my view that love is the primary goal of discipleship. After stating that we are to be holy as God is holy, Peter walks us through the story of God and how the Gospel of Jesus Christ that came through faith is our hope (1 Pet 1:18–21). And then he makes this incredible statement, "Now that you have purified yourselves by obeying the truth so that you have sincere love for each other, love one another deeply, from the heart. For you have been born again, not of perishable seed, but of imperishable, through the living and enduring word of God" (1 Pet 1:22–23). His reference to having been purified is a reference to the holiness we have in Christ through the Gospel. Our holiness is not through our obedience to the moral law or any other law. That is a misunderstanding of Peter's letter. It is through "obeying the truth" that we are pure and holy. The phrase "obedience to the Gospel" occurs several times in Scripture and never refers to obedience to moral law or living righteously. It always has to do with placing your faith in the finished work of Christ! (2 Thes 1:8; 1 Pet. 4:17). Peter's point about the impact of the Gospel and the righteousness given to us, which produces purity, is that we should love each other! The goal is "sincere love for each other, love one another deeply, from the heart!"

My purpose is not to write a theological treatise about the nature of God, but I would submit to you that this approach will not serve you well. You will become shipwrecked in legalism and moralism, not unlike the Pharisees. The defining attribute of disciples who follow Jesus is love. The Scripture says, "God is love. Whoever lives in love lives in God, and God in them" (1 Jn 4:16). This truth does not negate righteousness. We are not arguing against righteousness. We are simply saying that love is the central story and goal of discipleship. The reality is that righteousness is the result of loving. Jesus said, "Love the Lord your God with all your heart and with all your soul and with all your mind. This is the first and greatest commandment. And the second is like it: 'Love your neighbor as yourself.' All the Law and the Prophets hang on these two commandments." The whole law is fulfilled when we live a life of love. Remember, what we are talking about is a holy and righteous love. A disciple who is growing in love for God and others will necessarily be growing in righteous living. The converse is not true. You don't always get a loving people because they are growing in moral behavior. This speaks to the primacy of love.

> If we read the Scripture with a lens that the story of God is primarily about right living and righteousness, we will make our discipleship about right living and moral behavior.

The Fall in the garden changed the world. Man was created as an image bearer to reflect the love of God in the world. He chose not to love God but rebelled against him by choosing to eat of the tree of good and evil. The result was guilt and shame. Guilt and shame are relational terms that describe a broken love relationship. When God entered the garden after the Fall, Adam and Eve hid behind the foliage. Instead of displaying the glory of God, now they were hiding. Theologically, we could describe the effects of the Fall in many ways (total depravity, filth, bankruptcy). In relationship to love, they did not love God nor love others. The beautiful garden that was created for them out of the love of the Trinity, which was once safe and secure, was now dangerous. They experienced rejection. They chose to follow a way other than God to find meaning and purpose. As mankind multiplied, so did the effects of sin.

The story of God is the story of God lovingly pursuing man to renew the relationship that was broken in the garden. He reveals his plan of redemption in seed form in Genesis 3:15 and expands it in his covenant with Abraham (Gen. 12, 15, 17). He hears the cry of his people in Egypt and sends Moses to rescue them from slavery. The establishment of the law and the sacrificial system was all given as part of the plan of redemption that came from the heart of a loving God. However, all along, people rejected the love of God. If you read the book of Song of Solomon allegorically, you have a picture of the love of God for his bride. Hosea being instructed to go and marry a promiscuous woman named Gomer is another picture of this broken relationship that demonstrates God's faithful love and pursuit of an adulterous lover.

The story of God is centered on Jesus Christ, the Son of God who is sent by the Father to demonstrate the full extent of God's love. He is the seed promised to Abraham in Genesis, the Passover lamb in Exodus, the scapegoat in Leviticus, the Living Water in Numbers, the fulfillment of the Law in Deuteronomy, and on and on. The story of God is the story of a loving God pursuing man to redeem and restore a broken relationship. The story reaches the pinnacle when the Son is incarnated in human flesh and lives a perfect loving life. It is at the end of his life when he gives his perfect life as a substitutionary atonement for the sins of the world. Here we have the full expression of the love of God on display. Love is not selfish as it gives all for the sake of others. He endured the pain, was rejected, was ridiculed, and died the death of a criminal. None of this just happened to him. It was planned from the creation of the world (Eph 1:4). It was predicted in the Old Testament thousands of years before the event (Isa. 53, Ps. 22). Every detail was fulfilled as revealed by the prophets. This just didn't happen. It was meticulously planned by a loving God.

And after he laid down his life as a sacrifice, he rose again in victory. Sin and death were destroyed. Christ, the greatest lover of our soul, now intercedes for us at the right hand of God. The curtain that divided the holy place from the holy of holies was torn from top to bottom, and Jesus made a way for the unrighteous to approach God. No lambs were needed any longer. The lamb who takes away the sins of the world has provided a way once for all (Heb 10:14). Now we have fellowship with the Father and with the Son and with the Holy Spirit (1 Cor 1:9; 1 Jn 1:3; 2 Cor 13:15). Fellowship is the description of loving relationship we enjoy because of the finished work of Christ on the cross.

The book of Revelation gives us a glimpse into the future life we will have with the Godhead. It is here that we read about a great marriage supper of the lamb (Rev 19:9). The relationship of the redeemed, the church, is likened to that of a bride (also Eph 5:25). This is a love story.

It was the plan of God since creation for man to bear the image of God in the created world. The redemption of Christ has made this possible. A key passage in understanding God's plan is John 17:20–26. In the high priestly prayer of Jesus Christ, he prays for the image of God to be revealed to the world through his disciples:

> My prayer is not for them alone. I pray also for those who will believe in me through their message, that all of them may be one, Father, just as you are in me and I am in you. May they also be in us so that the world may believe that you have sent me. I have given them the glory that you gave me, that they may be one as we are one—I in them and you in me—so that they may be brought to complete unity. Then the world will know that you sent me and have loved them even as you have loved me. Father, I want those you have given me to be with me where I am, and to see my glory, the glory you have given me because you loved me

before the creation of the world. Righteous Father, though the world does not know you, I know you, and they know that you have sent me. I have made you known to them, and will continue to make you known in order that the love you have for me may be in them and that I myself may be in them.

Here Christ prays for the glory that belonged to the Father that was shared by the Son to be given to the disciples. The purpose of this shared glory is for the world to know the love of God and the Son's love. He prays for this love to be in them. This is the pure unadulterated love that was before the creation and Fall. The glory is the reflection of the supreme attribute of love! This is what Jesus prayed for when he was thinking about all those who would believe. The attribute in the disciples that would most convince the world that Jesus was the Son of God sent from the Father was love.

Peter makes an even stronger statement about how we can share in the divine love of God when he says, "Through these he has given us his very great and precious promises, so that through them you may participate in the divine nature having escaped the corruption in the world caused by evil desires" (1 Pet 1:4). We participate in the divine nature through the divine power that dwells within us through his Spirit. We reveal the love of God, and we grow in our love, thus, revealing the glory of God! Our nature was once for evil desires, but the promise is that "Christ in us" brings about a radical transformation. The chief reason for change is love. In fact, we will learn that love is what drives the change.

The story of God is a love story from beginning to end. Love is broken and destroyed. We have chosen to love another. It doesn't matter what or who, but we have rejected our lover. God has provided a way for that relationship to be reestablished. As disciples of Christ who have received the work of God by faith, our love for God is being made pure. This is the focus of discipleship.

Reflection Questions

1. When you tell the story of the Bible, is it a love story or a law story?

2. When you reflect on the attributes of God, where does love fall in the list? How might this impact your telling of the story of God?

3. The redemption story of the Bible is framed around the restoration of the creation. What is your understanding of the image of God in man? How does this shape your understanding of discipleship?

4. Read 1 John 4 and reflect on the centrality of love in the purposes of God in discipleship. Record how God speaks to you.

4

The Primacy
of Love

"Teacher, which is the great commandment in the Law?"
And he said to him, "You shall love the Lord your God with
all your heart and with all your soul and with all your mind.
This is the great and first commandment. And a second is
like it: You shall love your neighbor as yourself. On these two
commandments depend all the Law and the Prophets."

—Matthew 22:36–40

Jesus quoted at least twice from Deuteronomy 6:5 and adds further commentary not contained in Deuteronomy. Here is what Jesus said to the Sadducees and Pharisees, "Teacher, which is the greatest commandment in the Law?"[37] Jesus replied, "Love the Lord your God with all your heart and with all your soul and with all your mind. This is the first and greatest commandment. And the second is like it: Love your neighbor as yourself. All the law and the prophets hang on these two command-

> *In effect, Jesus was saying*
> *that if you understand*
> *these two commands*
> *about love, the rest of the*
> *Old Testament is simply*
> *an amplification of them.*

ments." Jews know this Scripture as the Shema (plus Deut 6:4: "The Lord our God is one God"). It was prayed twice a day, morning and evening, as

27

part of the daily prayer services. What Jesus added by way of commentary is that the law and the prophets hang on these two commands. The law and the prophets are the two divisions of the entire Old Testament. This was quite a statement. Now that is placing loving God and others in a prime place! This would have been especially offensive to the teachers of the law who prided themselves on doing the law with all its ceremonial trimmings. However, they couldn't object to the truth.

To love God with all your heart, soul, and mind (Jesus also uses "strength" when making this statement) is to love God completely. With every ounce of our being, we are to love God. We are to love no other. We are to have no other gods before him. Our passion is to be for God. If we live like this, we will reflect the glory of God we were created for. Remember, we are image bearers.

We are also to love our neighbor as ourselves. Jesus is not commanding us to love ourselves in this Scripture. He is helping us to understand the nature of love. Love is sacrificial and giving. It loves regardless of the cost. Jesus knows that we love ourselves too much. Most of our lives are spent protecting ourselves. This is our problem. Our passion is ourselves! Jesus was teaching us to love others and treat them like we would treat ourselves. We will give everything to protect ourselves. Do likewise for others. Paul agrees with Christ when he states in Galatians 5:14, "For the entire law is fulfilled in keeping this one command: 'Love your neighbor as yourself'."

> *"For the entire law is fulfilled in keeping this one command: 'Love your neighbor as yourself'."*
> (Galatians 5:14)

The second part (actually the first part, as it is recorded first) of the Shema is "the LORD our God is one God." The word in Hebrew for "one" is the word *ached*. Driver and Brown tell us that the word has several usages. It can mean the number one, as in one, two, three. It can also mean primary and the first. It also is used frequently to describe unity and togetherness. All of these apply to the Trinity. He is the one true God, and there are no others. He is one in that he is first and should be worshipped as such. The LORD is also unity. The context of the statement is about love (love the LORD your God...). Could it be that the idea of unity, or a God who is in perfect agreement, peace, love within himself is what is being emphasized?

The Trinity is always in loving relationship with one another. Jesus uses the truth of this kind of unity in John 17 in the high priestly prayer. Jesus said,

"I do not ask for these only, but also for those who will believe in me through their word, that they may all be one, just as you, Father, are in me, and I in you, that they also may be in us, so that the world may believe that you have sent me" (John 17:21–22). We are called to be one as the Trinity is one. It hardly makes sense that Jesus was teaching that we are like him in oneness, in substance. Actually, some cults use this passage to teach this heresy. The focus is unity and relationality. We cannot be dogmatic about this as we have few contextual clues, but it is an interesting idea that the people of God were to keep before themselves daily, and with their children, the idea that God lives in perfect love (Elohim is the plural used here to describe the LORD) and that we are to love him and others. He is our example of pure love. Jesus Christ affirmed this to the apostles and expanded on it as our example.

1 Corinthians 13:1–13

Perhaps the most familiar Scripture on the primacy of love is 1 Corinthians 13. It is a classic piece of literature even for the nonbeliever. It is often read at weddings as it certainly applies to the marriage relationship. But

> *Love is the greatest. It has primacy. If that is so, shouldn't it be the focus of our discipleship? Perhaps we should consider "the way of love."*

the context of the Scripture is a dysfunctional church that is abounding with moral failure and a lack of unity. Paul offers the "way of love" (1 Cor 14:1).

1 Corinthians 13:1–13 states,

If I speak in the tongues of men and of angels, but have not love, I am a noisy gong or a clanging cymbal. And if I have prophetic powers, and understand all mysteries and all knowledge, and if I have all faith, so as to remove mountains, but have not love, I am nothing. If I give away all I have, and if I deliver up my body to be burned, but have not love, I gain nothing. Love is patient and kind; love does not envy or boast; it is not arrogant or rude. It does not insist on its own way; it is not irritable or resentful; it does not rejoice at wrongdoing, but rejoices with the truth. Love bears all things, believes all things, hopes all things, endures all things. Love never ends. As for prophecies, they will pass away; as for tongues, they will cease; as for knowledge, it will pass away. For we know in part and we prophesy in part, but when the perfect comes, the partial will pass away. When I was a child, I spoke like a child, I thought like a child, I reasoned like a child. When I became a man, I gave up childish ways. For now we see in a mirror dimly, but then face to face. Now I know in part; then I shall know fully, even as I have been fully known. So now faith, hope, and love abide, these three; but the greatest of these is love.

The opening paragraph is a clear and compelling argument for the primacy of love in discipleship. Imagine a disciple who can speak in tongues, understands all mysteries and all knowledge, has so much faith that it can move mountains like Jesus said could be done, and that same person gives away everything they earn to the poor and lives sacrificially in hardship. I might be pleased with my disciple! In fact, I might even consider my discipling to be a complete success. But in God's economy, it amounts to nothing. Not a little. Not something that needs some love added. Not a smaller reward. Nothing. Nada. I don't know if Paul could have stated it more strongly. Love is everything.

There are four words used to describe love in the Greek language. Agape love is the one that is chosen to describe the love of God and the love we are to have for one another. It is the kind of love described here. It is not an emotional response or a good feeling but a decision to seek out the interest of others. Notice the descriptions and how each description is seeking the best for the other person. Love is patient—not getting what you want for yourself in a timely manner. Love is kind—does what is needed by the other person. Love does not envy—it isn't comparing oneself in hopes of getting ahead of someone else. Love doesn't boast—it boasts in others and lifts them up. It is not proud—it doesn't consider themselves better than others. It does not dishonor others—it finds a way to honor others. It is not self-seeking—it seeks the welfare of the other person. It is not easily angered—it is not protecting oneself or using others for their own gain. It keeps no record of wrongs—it forgives and covers over sin. Love doesn't delight in evil—it wants the best for others, even their enemies. It rejoices in the truth—it doesn't lie or deceive for personal gain, especially at the expense of others. It always protects—it acts to defend and watch over others. It always trusts—it believes the best of others. It

> *The truth is that we often are more concerned about a person's behavior than what is in their heart. To this Jesus objected.*

always hopes—it desires the best for others. It always perseveres—it doesn't give up on people but keeps pursuing the relationship.

Love never fails. Love is always important. It has its primacy both here and in heaven forever. This is unlike prophesy and knowledge. Both will not be needed in the age to come.

Isn't it interesting that faith, hope, and love are the things that are valued most? Even within the context, hope and faith are assumed in love.

Mark 7:14–23

So much of discipleship is learning to conform to the standards of the discipler. This was true of the Pharisees who were critical of Jesus and his disciples for not following the ceremonial traditions of the elders. Jesus was accused of eating food with defiled hands. I have been around this kind of thinking. Actually, we all have. Growing up in the seventies, it was the church thing to bash all rock music as evil because of the beat (the devil matches your heart rate with the drums, and you are hypnotized to do his bidding). Did you know that gum chewing was evil? Or what of movies and the theater? One church that was leasing space from our church wrote a scathing letter to our elder board for using a theater theme for vacation Bible school. We were promoting Satan's work, especially amongst the children. Our judgment was to have a millstone thrown around our neck and tossed into the sea. But not all judgment is that extreme.

> Again Jesus called the crowd to him and said, "Listen to me, everyone, and understand this. Nothing outside a person can defile them by going into them. Rather, it is what comes out of a person that defiles them." After he had left the crowd and entered the house, his disciples asked him about this parable. "Are you so dull?" he asked. "Don't you see that nothing that enters a person from the outside can defile them? For it doesn't go into their heart but into their stomach, and then out of the body." (In saying this, Jesus declared all foods clean.) He went on: "What comes out of a person is what defiles them. For it is from within, out of a person's heart, that evil thoughts come—sexual immorality, theft, murder, adultery, greed, malice, deceit, lewdness, envy, slander, arrogance and folly. All these evils come from inside and defile a person." (Mark 7:14–23)

The heart is what Jesus was concerned about. The heart is the source of defilement. That is why Ezekiel 36:26 prophesied the need for a new heart, "I will give you a *new heart* and put a *new* spirit in you; I will remove from you your *heart* of stone and give you a *heart* of flesh." When the writer was speaking of the heart, he was speaking about what drives a person. It refers to the passions of a person. The Pharisees were concerned with the outside behavior and not concerned with the heart. Jesus pointed this out specifically to the Pharisees by challenging their "evidence" of self-righteousness. The Pharisees would declare the portion of their income that they would use to help their mother and father and declare it corban, or devoted to God. They did this to avoid loving their parents!

The heart is evil and self-seeking. It desires everything opposite of the definition of love as given in 1 Corinthians 13. We need a new heart. A heart of love is required. If you want to disciple someone effectively, you will need to focus on the heart/soul. I believe discipleship of the soul is the only way to see real and deep change.

Philippians 2:1–5

The supreme example of love in Scripture is the love of Christ expressed in his submission to the cross. I have included this text for our consideration in understanding the primacy of love in discipleship because, ultimately, Jesus is our example. He shows us the way to love and how to be an image bearer of the love of God in our world. Philippians 2:15 says,

> Therefore if you have any encouragement from being united with Christ, if any comfort from his love, if any common sharing in the Spirit, if any tenderness and compassion, then make my joy complete by being like-minded, having the same love, being one in spirit and of one mind. Do nothing out of selfish ambition or vain conceit. Rather, in humility value others above yourselves, not looking to your own interests but each of you to the interests of the others.

Being united in Christ in his love necessarily requires us to be like-minded and to have the same love. The kenosis, or emptying, that Christ experienced as he left heaven with all of its benefits to lay down his life for us is seen as the supreme example of how to love. Perhaps this is what Jesus had in mind when he instructed his disciples to pick up their cross and follow him.

Paul was speaking about living a life of love that that requires humility. Andrew Murray adds to this concept of humility, "Here is the path to the higher life: down, lower down! Just as water always seeks and fills the lowest place, so the moment God finds men abased and empty, His glory and power flow in to exalt and to bless."[5] Humility takes the place that looks to the interest of others. St. Augustine said, "If you should ask me what are the ways of God, I would tell you that the first is humility, the second is humility, and the third is humility. Not that there are no other precepts to give, but if humility does not proceed all that we do, our efforts our meaningless."[6] Augustine saw humility as the characteristic of love from which all the other ones flow. Discipleship of the soul will emphasize this aspect of love called humility because it was modeled by our Savior. It gets to the core of love—leaving self-centeredness and self-interest behind for the sake of others.

> *John gives us the key for the transformation of a life. It is God's love.*
>
> *For John, true disciples are identified by love because that is the primary character of God. If you know the love of God, then you will love others.*

1 John 3 and 4

The apostle John was the one who reclined next to Jesus at the Last Supper. Whether you read his Gospel, his letters, or the Revelation, you can't but notice the theme of love. He was passionate for Christ. He writes as one who sees everything through the lens of love. He repeats the phrase "God is love" (1 Jn 4:8,16). You will be changed by the pure and holy love of the Father. That love was on full display when Christ came to die for our sins. John says,

> God is love. This is how God showed his love among us: He sent his one and only Son into the world that we might live through him. This is love: not that we loved God, but that he loved us and sent his Son as an atoning sacrifice for our sins. Dear friends, since God so loved us, we also ought to love one another. (1 John 4:8–12)

Love becomes known in the Gospel. God's pure love is revealed in the self-sacrifice of the Son. We observe impure love all the time in our world. Most of it is really love for self and the world. John identifies the false expressions of love early in his letter (1 John 2:15–16). It is consumed with self-gratification. We live for ourselves. It is at the cross that God's love cannot be ignored. It is all-consuming and life-changing. The "seed" of God is planted in the soul of man, and that seed sprouts love. It grows in greater and greater expressions of love. Why? Because that seed is Jesus the Son of God. He lives within you (1 John 3:9–10). When you receive and know the love of God, life can no longer go on as it did before. The love of God is now in your soul. Your soul has been changed. John says this is the very quality of a life that is the evidence of being known by God and knowing God: "We know that we have passed from death to life, because we love our brothers. Anyone who does not love remains in death" (1 John 3:14).

He tells us that we are to rely on love: "If anyone acknowledges that Jesus is the Son of God, God lives in them and they in God. And so we know and rely on the love God has for us. God is love. Whoever lives in love lives in God, and God in them." (1 John 3:15-16 NIV). We don't rely on our disciplines. It is the very love of God that we are to rely on. Love is what changes us. The pure love of God is transforming.

He continues by telling us that we don't need anything else to bring about our transformation. He says, "In this way, love is made complete" (1 John 4:17). The word that translated "complete" means that there is nothing lacking. It has the ability to bring about perfection. Love matures the believer to be like Christ. His love is able to purify us so that we have complete confidence on the day of judgment that we will be "like him" (1 John 4:17).

The opposite of love is fear. If we are not motivated by love or live as one who is fully loved (accepted, significant, and secure in Christ), we will live in fear. Fear is the state of mind that must seek out acceptance, significance, and security from the world. It causes the emotion of fear and anxiety because the world can't offer what God only can provide. The world's acceptance is always conditional. Significance is always related to our performance—our last performance. And security is only a myth in the world. Anything and everything can be taken away in an instant. Only the love of God can change all this. Our soul is changed and made perfect (pure) by the love of God. The result is a life that loves others for their sake rather than to meet our own needs of our soul. Love fills us up. The love of God satisfies (1 John 4:18).

There is a correspondence of knowing God's love and loving others. The key to love others begins and is developed by abiding in the love of God. This is why the mark of a disciple is love.

Ephesians 3:14–19

There are many other passages about the primacy of love in the Scriptures, but I will conclude this section with Paul's prayer for the church in Ephesus. Look at what Paul prays for,

> For this reason I kneel before the Father, from whom every family in heaven and on earth derives its name. I pray that out of his glorious riches he may strengthen you with power through his Spirit in your inner being, so that Christ may dwell in your hearts through faith. And I pray that you, being rooted and established in love, may have power, together

with all the Lord's holy people, to grasp how wide and long and high and deep is the love of Christ, and to know this love that surpasses knowledge—that you may be filled to the measure of all the fullness of God.

Paul spent more time in Ephesus than in any other city. He was intimate with the people and elders, having spent years discipling and teaching there. Ephesus was a gateway city to Asia Minor as it was the capital of the region and the key port from which both trade and thought was distributed to the world. Paul knew that the Ephesian church had great potential, but apart from the deep love of God bringing about transformation, they would fall prey to the devil's schemes. Later in the letter, he would write about spiritual warfare and weapon of prayer. Ephesus was the home of the god Artemis, but the entire city was carved with temples to the deities of that period. I have walked through that ancient city and was overwhelmed by the number of gods that were worshipped. Artemis was a deity who was a virgin and rejected marriage. Her representation, however, is that of a woman covered with breasts. It is a grotesque distortion of womanhood. She committed herself to hunting and nature. In this same city, prostitution was rampant. Even today, when you walk down the main street off the promenade that came from the harbor, there is a footprint carved in the stone pointing to the house of prostitution. Love in Ephesus was convoluted to say the least. In the midst of this, Paul preaches the Gospel of Christ. God raised up a church to be an image bearer of God's love in the quagmire of human filth.

> *The prayer of Paul for the Ephesians is focused on grasping the love of God. He describes this love as "wide and long and high and deep."*

There is a lifetime of learning when it comes to learning about the love of God! Paul believes that praying for them about growing in this knowledge of love is what will make the difference. Paul uses a metaphor of nature to explain the critical nature of grasping the love of God. He prays that they would be "rooted and established" in love. A tree is not strong enough to endure the strong winds that blow until the tree is rooted. This means that the tentacles of the tree that extend deep into the ground have become strong and extensive enough to support the tree. The stronger the roots, the more fruitful the tree will be. In an area that is arid and rocky, this allusion to the importance of roots would have been keenly understood. Disciples must be rooted in love. They must have their love nourished. It is then, and only then, that they may be "filled to the measure of all the fullness of God."

Reflection Questions

1. If love is truly primary, then should our goal of discipleship and mea-
    surement of progress of discipleship be love? How would this change
    the way we think about discipleship?

2. How would discipleship look different if our focus was on developing
    a soul that loved?

3. What does it mean to "to know this love that surpasses knowledge"
    (Eph 3)? What is Paul telling us about love and its importance?

4. How often do we pray the prayer of Paul for our disciples to know the
    depth, height, width of God's love? Why does Paul pray for this?

5

Sin Is Primarily Relational

And he answered, "You shall love the Lord your God with all your heart and with all your soul and with all your strength and with all your mind, and your neighbor as yourself."

—Luke 10:27

We have already demonstrated from the teachings of Christ that the command to love your God with all your heart, soul, mind, and strength and your neighbor as yourself, sums up the entire Law and the Prophets. If this is true, then sin (breaking of God's law) is primarily relational in nature. Ultimately, sin is so terrible because it violates the primary attribute of God. Remember, we were created to be image bearers

> *Law breaking is a heart issue. It is love issue. The issue is that you love something more than God and others.*

reflecting the glory of God. God is love. His love is pure (holy). It is perfect love. Love is closely related to goodness, and God always chooses to relate to us in a way that is for our good.

If we are to learn to disciple peoples' hearts to love God and love others, we need to be totally convinced that sin is relational in nature and not primarily moral. If our focus is in morality, we will not disciple the heart; we will address the breaking of law.

Jesus said the whole Old Testament revelation (Law and the Prophets) is subsumed in the commandments to love God and others. But it is the Ten Commandments that form our thinking about sin in our society. Let's take a brief look at the Ten Commandments and test the teaching of Christ about their relational nature. I have a feeling that Jesus was right about this!

It is important to recognize that the context of the giving of the Ten Commandments was that God had rescued Israel from slavery out of the hands of the Egyptians. For four hundred years, they were in bondage and slavery. But the story goes back further than that. God's act of love in freeing Israel goes back to his loving choice of a people to be image bearers. Adam and Eve failed to be image bearers, and the world tumbled down so far that God sent a great flood to destroy almost all of mankind to begin again. It wasn't too long after the flood that Noah and his descendants started down the same path.

Because God created man to bear his image and reflect his image to the world, he chose to establish a covenant with Abraham and his descendants to be that image bearer. Prior to the giving of the Ten Commandments, God speaks through Moses to the people, "Because he loved your ancestors and chose their descendants after them, he brought you out of Egypt by his Presence and great strength, to drive out before you nations greater and stronger than you and bring you into their land to give it to you for your inheritance, as it is today" (Deut 4:37–38). The Ten Commandments were given to a people of the covenant whom he loved. The people were to live in this covenantal love by living the Ten Commandments. God's love was driving his movement. He desired what was good for his people. Living in obedience to the Law was intended for their good. Listen to what Moses said to Israel immediately before reading the commandments to them: "Keep his decrees and commandments, which I am giving you today, so that it may go well with you and your children after you and that you may live long in the land the LORD your God gives you for all time" (Deut. 4:40). God's love is good. Live a life of love, and life will be good. God has in mind the return to the garden where love abounded before the Fall.

Of course, we understand that the nation of Israel didn't and couldn't live according to the law. This did not surprise God. In fact, God provided a sacrificial system at the same time he provided the law that would foreshadow Christ. Saving would not come through the law but through a loving God who dispenses grace. He had already promised this grace through faith to Abraham and that it would come through his seed. As Galatians points out:

> Why, then was the law given at all? It was added because of transgressions until the Seed to whom the promise referred had come…Is the Law, therefore, opposed to the promises of God? Absolutely not! For if a law had been given that could impart life, then righteousness would certainly have come by the law. (Gal 3:19, 21)

The commandments served as a taskmaster to teach us of our failings and need of a savior. Through the seed, Christ, we would learn how to live love and be an image bearer.

The first four commandments refer to how the people of the covenant were to love God. The second six commandments refer to how the people were to love one another. Here are the first four commandments:

> I am the Lord your God, who brought you out of Egypt, out of the land of slavery. You shall have no other gods before me. You shall not make for yourself an image in the form of anything in heaven above or on the earth beneath or in the waters below. You shall not bow down to them or worship them; for I, the Lord your God, am a jealous God, punishing the children for the sin of the parents to the third and fourth generation of those who hate me, but showing love to a thousand generations of those who love me and keep my commandments. You shall not misuse the name of the Lord your God, for the Lord will not hold anyone guiltless who misuses his name. Observe the Sabbath day by keeping it holy, as the Lord your God has commanded you. Six days you shall labor and do all your work, but the seventh day is a Sabbath to the LORD your God. On it you shall not do any work, neither you, nor your son or daughter, nor your male or female servant, nor your ox, your donkey or any of your animals, nor any foreigner residing in your towns, so that your male and female servants may rest, as you do. Remember that you were slaves in Egypt and that the Lord your God brought you out of there with a mighty hand and an outstretched arm. Therefore the Lord your God has commanded you to observe the Sabbath day.

The first commandment to "have no other God before me" is a command to love God more than anyone or anything else. It is a command to find life in God himself. It is surely a warning about idolatry, which was rampant in the land; but it was more than that. Man was created to worship, and if God were not worshipped, surely he would worship other things. He would seek life in things that could not provide what is only available in God himself. It was a call to an intimate love relationship and exclusive commitment. Pure love. A holy love. It is God alone who is committed to your welfare. The commandment is prefaced by the statement, "I am the LORD your God, who brought you out of Egypt, out of the land of slavery." He is good. He is the good shepherd.

The second commandment, like the first, is a call to love God exclusively. No image is to be made to bow down to like those in the land of Palestine. This is a call to pure love. God is a jealous God. Not that God is insecure or weak, but rather, he wants for us to enjoy him and reflect the glory of his image alone. Romans 1:22–23 tells us that "although they claimed to be wise, they became fools and exchanged the glory of the immortal God for images made to look like a mortal human being and birds and animals." The glory of God cannot be displayed through images of creation. Only loving human beings who are image bearers can reflect that glory as they love God with everything they have with complete exclusivity.

The third commandment instructs us to love God by not misusing his name. Respect is the cornerstone of good relationships. The quality of our relationship with God depends on the love and regard we have for Him. It also depends on the way we express respect for Him in the presence of others. We are expected always to honor who and what He is. Conversely, the use of God's name in a flippant, disrespectful manner, expresses an attitude that disdain the relationship we are supposed to have with him. This can vary from careless disregard to hostility and antagonism. It covers misusing God's name in any way.

The fourth commandment is to keep a Sabbath day of rest. At first glance, this command seems to have little to do with love of God. It is also the most ignored commandment in the Christian church today, although there is a growing sense of importance to this commandment. It should be noticed that it was the regular custom of Jesus himself to observe the Sabbath (Luke 4:16). This was also true of the apostles (Acts 17:2; 18:4).

The Sabbath is vital to our relationship with God.

The Sabbath is vital to our relationship with God because it shapes the way we perceive and worship Him. We should remember the Sabbath by formally worshiping God on that day. Otherwise, we forfeit that special understanding that God wants to develop in us by worshiping Him on that day. It is by ceasing our normal labor and activities that we are reminded of an essential lesson every week. After six days of fashioning this beautiful earth and everything in it, our Creator ceased molding the physical part of His creation and rested on the seventh day. (Genesis 2:1–3) (the-ten-commandments.org).[7]

The other recording of the Ten Commandments in Exodus 20 gives the basis of keeping the Sabbath; it is remembering God as our creator. We live our lives by following his way of resting every seventh day. However, in Deuteronomy, the reason given is that God was the one who brought Israel out of slavery from Egypt. It is an appeal to a deeper relationship based on the loving acts of God toward us. If the Sabbath is kept for other reasons other than pursuing a loving relationship with God, the purpose of the commandment is not being fulfilled.

The final six commandments are focused on our love for other people. If you don't honor your parents, or commit murder, or steal, or lie, or covet what other people have, you are not living out a life of love. You are living selfishly. You are putting your own desires above those of others. It is true that life would be better if people lived like this, but the underlying principle that undergirds righteous living is the love that we are called to reflect as image bearers.

Even though the final six commandments are directed at our love for others, it should be noted that each one of these commandments also have to do with our love for God. They are not exclusively related to the love of others. For instance, if you commit murder, you are destroying the creation of God who was created to be an image bearer. You are failing to love God when you destroy his creation and fail to value that which God loves. If you commit adultery and divorce, you violate the plan of God for his image bearers to reflect the glory of God as he intended (male and female he created them). Jesus said,

> "Haven't you read," he replied, "that at the beginning the Creator made them male and female," and said, "For this reason a man will leave his father and mother and be united to his wife, and the two will become one flesh'? So they are no longer two, but one flesh. Therefore what God has joined together, let no one separate." (Matt. 19:4–6)

Any variance from God's plan is an offense to God directly, not just to the person involved in the marriage. The same could be said about stealing, lying, and coveting. These are all offenses against God and his supreme love for us. Sin breaks our relationship with a holy God.

If you don't have this understanding of the final six commandments and their offense to the love of God, you will not understand David's confession after he broke five of the six commandments just discussed. He was on his rooftop when he saw the beauty of Bathsheba as she was bathing at her home. At that moment, he coveted his neighbor's wife. He sent for her and committed adultery with her. It was discovered that Bathsheba was pregnant, so to cover his sin, he brought back Uriah the Hittite, the husband of Bathsheba, to visit and sleep with her in hopes that he will believe the baby conceived was his. However, Uriah would not go into his wife while the rest of the army was at battle, so David's plan failed. It failed twice. Even after getting Uriah drunk, he would not violate the honor of his comrades on the battlefield and enjoy his wife while they were risking their lives (something David should have been doing as well). So David orchestrated the murder of Uriah through Joab. To cover up the murder, an elaborate deception and lie was told about how his death came to pass. David's love for himself was so great that he was willing to violate five of the Ten Commandments to please himself. This was a terrible sin against Uriah and Bathsheba. But that is not how David frames his sin.

God calls on Nathan the Prophet to rebuke David of his sin. Nathan tells a story about a poor man with a pet lamb that had become like a daughter to him. He had little else in life, but he cherished this lamb. Now there was a rich man who had many cattle and sheep, but instead of slaughtering one of his own sheep to eat, he takes the pet lamb from the poor man and slaughters it. David was furious at the rich man when he heard the story! David walked right into the trap laid for him by the prophet. Nathan than said, "You are the man!" (2 Sam 12:7).

David's response as recorded in 2 Samuel 12 to Nathan was "I have sinned against the LORD." His confession was not that he had sinned against Uriah and Bathsheba but the LORD himself. If the fifth through the tenth commandments were only about living in love for people, this confession would make little sense. David actually makes an even stronger statement in Psalm 51 when he writes a psalm about his confession. It is a beautiful expression of a fully repentant heart that understands his utter sinfulness and sinful nature from birth. Day and night, he is tormented by his sin ("always before me"). But then he makes this outrageous statement, "Against you, you only, have I sinned and done what is evil in your sight; so you are right in your verdict and justified when you judge." Wow! Is David totally oblivious to the offense against the family of Uriah? I don't think so. I believe that David was fully aware of his offense and the damage he had caused by his sin. Yet his perspective as indicated both in his response to Nathan and in Psalm 51 reflects an even greater burden that he had in relationship to his LORD. He realizes that ultimately God is his judge. It is the holy love of God that he has broken. He employs a literary device called hyperbole where he overstates the fact to make his point. He is not denying the offense to those he injured. He is expressing the prime importance of his relationship with God that has been offended by his sin. Ultimately, all sin is relational, and all sin is against God.

Cornelious Plantinga in his book, <u>Not the Way It's Supposed to Be: A Breviary of Sin,</u> states this truth with other words.[8] The premise of his book is that sin is breaking shalom. Shalom is the Hebrew idea of wholeness and peace. It is when everything is good or the way God designed life to be. Shalom is broken or lost when sin entered the world. Every time we commit sin, shalom is destroyed. Love is the only way shalom can be restored. It is God's way. It is the way made by Christ on the cross. When we walk as Jesus walked, we love like him.

> *Christ came to restore relationships and establish shalom. He is the bridge that makes that possible.*

Discipleship must focus on love because the goal of discipleship is to be image bearers of our God who is pure love. All sin is relational. We make a mistake when we focus discipleship on moral living. Moral living is a result of a pure and loving heart toward God and others. The entire Law and the Prophets are subsumed under the law to love the LORD will all our heart, soul, mind, and strength and our neighbor as thyself.

Campus Crusade popularized the bridge illustration to help us understand the implications of sin. Sin is represented by a deep and wide chasm. The loving and holy God is on one side of the chasm, and we (sinners) are on the other side. Only Christ himself could "bridge" the gap between God and man. This illustration has helped hundreds of thousands of people understand the work of Christ on the cross as he paid the penalty for our sin. That chasm, that is, a problem, is really a broken relationship. The chasm between God and us is of the same nature of that which exists between a husband and wife who divorce and have no relationship. Sin is relational. And because it is relational, it impacts our relationships.

Peter wrote about the relational nature of sin when he spoke about the relationship between a man and his wife. He gives instruction about how a man is to relate to his wife, "Husbands, in the same way be considerate as you live with your wives, and treat them with respect as the weaker partner and as heirs with you of the gracious gift of life, so that nothing will hinder your prayers" (1 Pet 3:7). Peter is pointing out how to love your wife well but in the process points out something very important. He indicates that not loving your wife breaks our relationship with God himself. Prayers are hindered when we sin. Fellowship with God is somehow interrupted in such a way that the most intimate way we connect with God is broken (prayer). Sin is relational.

The temptation to deal with discipleship from the perspective of moral living, law keeping, and good works is so pervasive that it shapes the way we read the Word of God. A very familiar Scripture is Matthew 7:21–23:

> Not everyone who says to me, "Lord, Lord," will enter the kingdom of heaven, but only the one who does the will of my Father who is in heaven. Many will say to me on that day, "Lord, Lord, did we not prophesy in your name and in your name drive out demons and in your name perform many miracles?" Then I will tell them plainly, "I never knew you. Away from me, you evildoers!"

Dan Delzell of *The Christian Post* notes that this passage is often used to get people to do more and better works for God. It is pointed out that only those who actually do the will of the Father in heaven are true disciples.[9] But the point of Jesus's teaching is actually very different. He says plainly, "I never knew you." The word *know* is a relational term. The issue for Jesus is one of relationship—genuine relationship. You can do all kinds of deeds without a relationship. That is why Jesus can say to those who did ministry in his own name that he never knew them. His focus was on the relationship because everything springs from this relationship, including good works. It is the context of a loving relationship that our hearts are transformed, and we respond in love to others.

> *That need is deep and drives us. That thirst can only be quenched by a loving God.*

On the way to Galilee, Jesus chose to go through Samaria and stopped in a town called Sychar. The name of the town seems to be related to the word *sepulcher*, as the two words sound similar. This is the location where Joseph's bones were laid to rest and is a holy location. A place of worship at Mt. Gerizim was just a thousand yards from this source of nourishment called Jacob's well. It was here that Jesus had a conversation with a woman who was thirsty and drawing water from the well. Jesus engaged her in conversation about water, requesting a drink. This led to a life-changing exchange that would impact not only her, but also her whole village.

As human beings, we have a thirst that must be satisfied with drink. We can't live without water. In the same way as spiritual beings designed to be image bearers, we are designed for what Jesus called living water. Without this water, we are lost. But we are thirsty. We have a need. That need is deep and drives us. That thirst can only be quenched by a loving God.

Ecclesiastes 3:11 says, "He has also set eternity in the human heart." This is another way of describing this deep thirst that only a loving relationship with God can fill. It drives us to pursue something to fill that void in the heart. If one thing does not work, then we find another. We are just hoping that the next thing will not disappoint us. There must be something or someone who can quench the never-ending thirst that just won't go away. It makes us restless and reckless. We are willing to do whatever it takes to find an answer, a reason, a purpose, a filling, a satisfaction.

The woman at the well had five husbands, and none of them filled that void. She was still thirsty. So thirsty was this woman that she was now living with another man trying to dowse her dryness. She didn't know what she was looking for—only that she hadn't found it.

And there was Jesus, standing right in front of her. He was the living water. On the last day of the Feast of Tabernacles, the priest would draw water before the people and pour it on the ground. When this happened, Jesus came forward and declared, "If anyone is thirsty, let him come to Me and drink." He who believes in Me, as the Scripture said, 'From his innermost being will flow rivers of living water'" (John 7:37–38). What this woman was looking for, and all human beings are searching for, is found nowhere else but in Jesus Christ, the Son of God. Only through him can our thirst be quenched, and once we do, we will look for no other substitute. Nothing will do.

The metaphor of thirst is described as a deep desire, a longing that has not been met. It is not met by religion, experience, achievement, or other men (as the woman at the well discovered). Only the lover of the universe can satisfy. We were designed by God for relationship with the all-loving creator God. And we were designed to glorify God by being an image bearer of that perfect love.

Reflection Questions

1. If we really believed that sin was first of all relational and not moral, how would that change how we disciple? Parent?

2. If the Ten Commandments were intended not to help us to live righteously, but to point out our failure to love both God and our fellow man, what place does the Ten Commandments have in discipleship?

3. How is discipleship related to "image bearing"?

4. The soul is thirsty for something. It is striving after something it is missing. How have you seen this in your own life, and how has it kept you from finding your fulfillment in Christ?

6

Substitutes for Living Water

*For my people have committed two evils: they have forsaken
me, the fountain of living waters, and hewed out cisterns
for themselves, broken cisterns that can hold no water.*

—Jeremiah 2:13

Like the woman at the well (John 4), the search to drench our thirst moves/
draws us to alternatives or substitutes for the real thing. Jesus looks deep
into her heart and recognizes that she is trying to find meaning and purpose
in life through a man. He knows she has had many men in her life, and none
of them brought satisfaction. Her soul was still disoriented. We don't know
we are searching in the wrong places, but our passion drives us forward. The
story of the Old Testament is the story of a people who chose substitutes to
the covenantal God of love.

The prophet Ezekiel condemned the nation of Israel for their failure to
love the LORD with all their heart. Here is what is recording in Scripture,

> Some of the elders of Israel came to me and sat down in front of me. Then
> the word of the LORD came to me: Son of man, these men have set up

idols in their hearts and put wicked stumbling blocks before their faces. Should I let them inquire of me at all? Therefore, speak to them and tell them, 'This is what the Sovereign LORD says: When any Israelite sets up idols in his heart and puts a wicked stumbling block before his face and then goes to a prophet, I the LORD will answer him myself in keeping with his great idolatry. I will do this to recapture the hearts of the people of Israel, who have all deserted me for their idols.' Therefore, say to the house of Israel, 'This is what the Sovereign LORD says: Repent! Turn from your idols and renounce all your detestable practices!' (Ezek. 14:1–6)

When we think about idols, we normally think of Asherah poles and golden calves. We immediately picture in our minds physical objects of worship. Ezekiel helps us gain a fuller understanding of our problem. The issue is really in our hearts. Remember that when the Scripture is talking about the heart, it is talking about our motivations, particularly related to love. What do we desire more than God in our hearts?

We find several stories in the Old Testament that illustrate this truth, but the one most familiar is the story of Achan in Joshua 7:7–26. Israel was soundly defeated at Ai. When Joshua inquired of the Lord why they lost the battle, God informed him that Israel has sinned and broken the covenant that was given to them. He even told Joshua that "they have even taken some of the accursed things, and have stolen and deceived and they have also put it among their own stuff." The man who was identified as the culprit was Achan. His sin of idolatry affected the entire nation. Achan did confess. This is what he said: "I have sinned against the LORD God of Israel, and this is what I have done. When I saw among the spoils a beautiful Babylonian garment, two hundred shekels of silver, and *a* wedge of gold weighing fifty shekels, I

> *I wonder what kind of idols we have hidden under our tents? (in our hearts?)*

coveted them and took them. And there they are, hidden in the earth in the midst of my tent, with the silver under it" (Jos 7:20–21).

One problem that we have is that we are not always aware of our idols. We confess with our mouth that Jesus is Lord, but we live and are motivated by so many things that have nothing to do with the Lordship of Christ. Do you recognize some of these idols that lurk in the earth beneath our tents? Do we seek comfort, approval, control, or power? All of these can become idols that drive our passion and energy. Here are some more idolatries: approval idolatry, helping idolatry, work idolatry, materialism idolatry, experience idolatry (always desiring new experiences and travel), and political idolatry.

Even good things can become idols, like ministry idolatry. It may look good on the outside, but buried beneath the earth, there are motivations that are so far from God. Ministry can be done for so many motivations other than for the love of God and love of people. When the ministry becomes difficult, these pastors tend to get angry and take it out on the sheep. The pressure forces that which is on the inside to come out. Yet so few of these pastors can point to their own tent and say exactly what is buried there that is destroying the community. They are totally deceived and unaware. They are quick to point out the sin of others (remember David condemning the rich man who took the pet lamb from the poor man?).

Family idolatry is a new kind of idolatry that has risen in the past fifty years. Perhaps it was always there, as we have placed our children in places of greater value than God. But it has been amped up in the culture, and it has society's blessing. Who can argue with focusing on the family? God tested Abraham with this kind of idolatry when he asked him to take his one and only son Isaac and sacrifice him on mount Moriah. Abraham passed that test.

Discipleship will require the uncovering of idols. That which is buried under the tent is destroying the church. It has impact on the entire community of faith. David Powlison has what he called X-ray questions to help with these important discipleship issues of the heart.[10] They are excellent for helping us to identify idols of the heart/soul. Ultimately, we are searching for answers to the following

> *"Describe a time in your life when you experienced great joy and felt great about yourself?" and "Describe an event where you experienced the great pain and how you responded to it?"* (Dr. Larry Crabb)

questions: What do we love? What things bring us acceptance, significance, and security other than the pure love of God?

Dr. Larry Crabb, in his training on spiritual direction, recommends two critical questions to explore with your disciples.[11] He calls these questions (and other versions of them) life-and-death stories. These two stories reveal what the heart is tempted to idolize and what we tend to protect ourselves from. Protection is also a form of idol worship. These are life-shaping experiences that have a lifelong impact on how we see the world.

I can recount several meaningful stories of joy growing up. Generally, I had a happy childhood and then high school happened. I won't bore you with all the details, but in my freshman year, I went out for the high school baseball team. I was always a good athlete, but I had a slight build (I was skinny and of average size). I held the record for batting average in the local Little League and played All-Stars, so I felt confident in my abilities. So when the posting of the team took place and I wasn't on it, I was not just disappointed but furious. There were at least eight others on the list who were a lot worse than me! Half the people on the list came to me and said the same thing and were shocked that I wouldn't be their teammate. How could the coach be that blind and stupid?

The following year, I announced to my parents that I was going to try out for the team again. Training started a few weeks before Easter break. I worked hard and was determined to make the team. My parents announced at the dinner table that they were going to take us on a three-week family vacation to Florida, including a trip to Disney. I knew this was going to be a problem, and sure enough, the coach made it clear that if I went on the trip, I wouldn't make the team. There was no guarantee that I would make the team if I stayed either. I decided to stay. It took lots of arm-twisting of my parents to leave a fifteen-year-old at home for three weeks, but I stayed and made the team. It was a great feeling. I worked hard, and I was rewarded. I was valued. I was valued for my performance and working hard. I liked that feeling. I have been living like that ever since. As I look back on my life, I can see a pattern that developed where achievement was driving my behavior, even my ministry. Love was in the mix less than I would admit. I am still learning about what drives my soul. As a disciple, I need the body of Christ to help me learn to live out of love for God and others rather than myself.

> So much of our lives are driven by our life-and-death stories rather than the love of God.

My death story takes me all the way back to when I was ten years old and was playing accordion for my neighborhood Bible club. Stop laughing! I've heard every joke ever created about accordions. My favorite is the Far Side cartoon that has an accordion band welcoming people into hell! Actually, playing the accordion at that age and leading the singing was not my death experience. It actually made me feel valuable (the achievement idol was already kicking in). My death experience was when the leader of the club made a fool out of me before the entire club (forty kids) because I got one word wrong in the memorization of the weekly verse. I believe it was the word *a*. It should have been *the*. The leader decided to make an example of me before everyone about not working hard and just glancing at the verse prior to coming to the club. I was horrified. I felt blood rushing into my face and my adrenaline firing up. I ran out the door and slammed the door so hard I thought I had broken the window. I remember telling myself over and over again as I walked down the street with clenched fists that I would never ever let that happen to me again. Shame took hold.

Death to me is being embarrassed and made fun of. Failure is not an option. This idol keeps me from attempting things that could end poorly. It prevents me from obedience to the loving requests of the Father. I make too many decisions on the basis of whether or not failure is a possibility. It is a battle for my soul.

We learn to say the right things and do the right things to convince others that we are disciples of Christ. The reality is that we have been mastered by idols of the heart. What is worse is that many of us don't know that it is happening. We are like King David pointing the finger at the rich man who took the poor man's pet lamb for his dinner but didn't see the problem in our own lives.

Reflection Questions

1. Reflect and write down your life-and-death stories. How do these sto-
    ries help you to understand the cravings of your soul?

2. What "good" things in our lives have the potential to grow into idols
    of the heart (I must have these to be satisfied)?

3. It is possible (probable) that we have idols beneath our tents that are
    hidden, but we have no awareness of these. If this is true of ourselves,
    it may also be true of others. How can we discover and dig up these
    idols that control us and keep us from fully loving our God?

4. What would disciple making look like if going after idols in the soul
    was critical, as they hinder us from full love for our Savior?

7

Vision for a Church That Loves

For the whole law can be summed up in a single commandment,
namely, "You must love your neighbor as yourself."

—Galatians 5:14

What would the church look like if discipleship was focused on the love/ passions of the soul? We have been created for the purpose of being an image bearer. What if our lives reflected more the glory of God that was expressed in the full extent of Christ's love demonstrated on the cross?

In every leadership course or book that I have ever read, I have been told that vision drives behavior. Now I know that this teaching is only partially true. It is the passions of the soul (we will discover shortly that the passions are simply different ways we experience and desire love) that drive behavior. However, when you cast vision, you are appealing to the soul and painting a picture of a desirable outcome. If that outcome connects with the soul, people will work toward that vision.

Jesus was a master at casting a vision for disciples who would love. He lived in a world that valued law keeping and right behavior. Discipleship of the Pharisees and Sadducees were firmly grounded in behavior conformity. His graphic imagery of whitewashed tombs and cups that were clean on the outside but filthy on the inside were designed to create a visceral reaction (Matt. 23:25). Is our discipleship creating death or just the appearance of life? My stomach turns if I think about drinking from a cup that has been sitting on the counter with rotting food and molds on the inside, no matter how clean it looks on the outside (Matt. 23:27). Jesus was casting vision for discipling the inside of a man—the soul.

Jesus challenged those who thought they were image bearers because they were living on the outside with some degree of conformity with expectations. That is the whole message of the Sermon on the Mount. Jesus takes the law that was the basis of their understanding of what it means to be a disciple and opens their eyes to see the heart issues beneath the surface. He even goes as far as to say, "I tell you that unless your righteousness surpasses that of the Pharisees and the teachers of the law, you will certainly not enter the kingdom of heaven" (Matt. 5:20). Righteousness that does not come from a heart of love is not righteousness at all!

One by one, he unpacks his thesis that discipleship must grab the heart. Just because you haven't murdered anyone doesn't mean you are righteous. If you are angry with your brother or sister, you haven't begun to fulfill the vision of God for an image bearer (Matt. 5:22). You think you are doing pretty well by not committing adultery? Not so fast. If you look at another woman with lust in your heart, you haven't begun to fulfill the vision of God for an image bearer (Matt. 5:28). Are you seeing the thrust of Jesus's teaching? He is after the motivation of the soul. He isn't impressed with the outside of the cup.

Are you convinced? Jesus doesn't stop there. He keeps hammering away lest we fail to get the point. The law says don't bear false witness. But you have figured out how to hedge the truth with oaths that have degrees of reliability. Why do you do this? It is because your heart is messed up. You find a way to obey without truly being an image bearer. An image bearer would simply say yes or no. Love is honest and doesn't deceive your brother or sister (Matt. 5:33–37).

> *Jesus isn't interested in making people better. His vision isn't for nice.*

Jesus doesn't beat around the bush. He hits us between the eyes. He gets right after it. "You have heard that it was said, Love your neighbor and hate your enemy. But I tell you, love your enemies and pray for those who persecute you, that you may be children of your Father in heaven" (Matt. 5:43–45). Jesus uses the phrase "children of your Father in heaven" to describe a true image bearer. You see, God causes rain to fall on both the righteous and the unrighteous. He loves all men. It isn't okay to just love those who love you or treat you well. Image bearers look differently from everyone else because they love those who don't love them back! The kind of love that God is developing in his image bearers is perfect. "Be perfect, therefore, as your heavenly Father is perfect" (Matt. 5:48). He is not talking about being perfect in behavior (moral living) but being perfect in your soul/heart. The Greek word used is *telios*, which signifies maturity, completeness, wholeness, and purity. The vision Jesus has for his disciples is a pure heart.

We will not go through the entire Sermon on the Mount, but it must be read with the vision of Christ in mind. If the heart is pure, reflecting the love of God, life will be much different from the world. Your prayer life will change, the way you care for your soul, the way you look at money and stuff will all shift in significant ways. These are heart issues. Jesus said, "No one can serve two masters. Either you will hate the one and love the other or you will be devoted to the one and despise the others" (Matt. 6:24). He was talking about money, but the truth applies to every area of life. God wants our hearts.

Jesus goes on to teach us that loving God is reasonable and attractive. Why not put your full trust in the one who loves you? Look at how he clothes the fields. And are you not more valuable than they are? (Matt. 6:28–32). Those who love God and seek his kingdom have the storehouse of God at their disposal just by asking! (Matt. 7:7–11).

The vision that Jesus has for his disciples is not for everyone. Few will get it. Few will find it. The road is very narrow and the gate that opens to the road is very small. The way of the heart is the pathway of discipleship (Matt. 7:13–14). We can join Christ in pointing people in the direction of the narrow road and the tiny little gate. The gate isn't locked. It is just not that easy to find. The other road is easy and is well travelled. In the end, though, there is disappointment. It will not get us to where we want to go.

Has the church settled for the broad road? The broad road is about outside-cup teaching and discipling. It teaches principles for living. It helps people live in such a way that is nicer. It is strong in teaching the law and prophets but misses the point. There is little or no attention to the soul. The focus of the church is getting more people in the chairs. Success is hardly ever measured by what is going on in the heart of the disciples. What is going on in the heart of man? That is where the battle is. Satan is waging war for the affections of man. Where in the church is there heart surgery going on? Soul talk? Do we even understand the passions of the soul?

Jesus ends the Sermon on the Mount with the parable of the wise and foolish builders. The foolish builder built his house on the sand while the wise man built his house on the rock. When the houses were completely erected, there was a torrential storm. The streams became rivers, and the winds blew with a mighty force. When the storm was over, the house on the sand "fell with a great crash" (Matt. 7:27). The key to understanding this parable is located in the introduction to the parable: "Therefore everyone who hears these words of mine and puts them into practice is like a wise man who built his house on the rock" (Matt. 7:24). Jesus is warning us not just to hear the revelation he is giving but to put them into practice. What words is he talking about? The connective "therefore" indicates that this parable is the conclusion of the Sermon of the Mount. His words are not a general warning about obeying Scripture but specific to the content of the sermon he just gave. He was contrasting the way of love with the religious communities' approach to discipleship. The question we must ask ourselves is what are we going to do about addressing the soul/heart of man in how we make disciples in the church?

Bernard of Clairvaux (1090–1153) describes four types of love. I think it is helpful in our understanding of having a vision for discipling people to grow and mature in the pure love of God. He developed a four-stage progression of love development as follows:

1. Love self for our own sake.
2. Love God for our own sake.
3. Love God for his sake.
4. Love ourselves for God's sake.[12]

We all begin in the first stage. It is the natural state of man since the Fall. We love ourselves. We love ourselves and are passionate about things that advance ourselves. That which makes us secure, significant, and accepted are pursued without blushing or restriction. We are self-consumed and even narcissistic. We use other people to feel loved. I am number one. Even the nice things we do for others are done because they make me feel better about myself. The Holy Spirit has not yet drawn me to himself. I am drifting at the whims of my empty self, trying to discover how to fill the void in my heart. All I know is that I feel better, at least for a time, when I do certain things. We are never truly satisfied as the foundation of acceptance, significance, and security (three passions of the soul) must be extracted from other people. Right and wrong is weighed by what brings temporary satisfaction to the passions of the soul. There is a thirst for something that is missing that God may use to draw me to himself.

In the second stage, we love God for our own sakes. This is the stage where we are awakened to the love of God and his great benefits. However, we love

God selfishly. We love God for what we can get from him—eternal life, for-giveness of sin, healing of our bodies, comfort in times of distress, promises of prayer. We begin our fellowship with God, but our desires are still for our own comfort. We taste God and know he is good. We trust him to a point because we still have an agenda. In this stage, we tend to use God to advance our own dreams and hopes. Nevertheless, our soul has been touched by the loving grace of God, and we have begun our journey of being an image bearer.

The third stage is when we love God for his sake. We become aware of our selfishness and yield ourselves more fully to God's desires and his ways. We have learned that our acceptance, significance, and security can be placed in God's hands. We become free to love others rather than trying to extract love out of others. God's love brings us greater freedom to love. We begin to love in ways that require self-denial and sacrifice. It is at this stage that the world can see a difference from how others live. The image of God in man is becoming clearer. It has no resemblance to that of unregenerate man.

The fourth and final stage is to love self for God's sake. This is the stage where we are now image bearers reflecting the love of God, as Christ modeled for us. The soul is no longer selfish but is only motivated by the pure love of God. There is no striving for acceptance, significance, or security because God's love has provided everything we need. Now we are free to provide that same acceptance, significance, and security to others. We are at rest without a demanding spirit because the soul is doing what it was created for. We can say we love ourselves because we are in harmony with God's loving nature.

Bernard describes this final stage:

O chaste and holy love! O sweet and gracious affection! O pure and cleansed purpose, thoroughly washed and purged from any selfishness, and sweetened by contact with God's will! To reach this state is to be-come godlike. As a drop of water poured into wine loses itself, and takes the color and savor of wine; or as a bar of iron, heated red—hot, be-comes like fire itself, forgetting its own nature; or as the air, radiant with sun—beams, seems not so much to be lit as to be light itself; so for those who are holy all human affections melt away by some incredible muta-tion into the will of God.[13]

Bernard didn't believe that this final stage was possible, with the excep-tion of brief and passing moments in this life. This is the state of love that is reserved for life when we see Christ face-to-face. 1 John 3:1 says:

See what great love the Father has lavished on us, that we should be called the children of God! The reason the world doesn't not know us is that did not know him. Dear friends, now we are children of God, and what we will be has not yet been made known. But we know that when Christ appears, we shall be like him, for we shall see him as he is. All who have this hope in him purify themselves, just as he is pure.

Pure love is produced by dwelling and focusing on our loving Savior. We need a vision that will address our souls.

The four stages of love as given by Bernard is a helpful paradigm as we envision discipleship in the church. The stages are not meant to be distinct categories but descriptions of points on the continuum of growing in the love of God. It helps us in two ways. First, it assists us in understanding that growing in love will be progressive, like a baby growing into adulthood. Patience will be required. Remember that God is patient with us and that he will complete his work. Second, it is beneficial because it identifies for us what to look for in the life of the disciple and what needs to be refined.

> I have dream of disciples whose soul has been so impacted by the love of God that they are free to love as God loves. The true mark of a disciple is one who loves like Jesus.

Imagine a church filled with disciples who love like what Bernard describes in stages 3 and 4? This is why I wrote this book. All other markers are imitations of the real thing. You can know your Bible and not love. You can be a great theologian and be a poor lover of people. I've seen people worship God and curse out people in the parking lot. Let us echo the words of Jesus when he said that you can prophesy, cast out demons, and perform miracles and none of these mean anything (Matt. 7:22–23). Being a great leader who attracts thousands of people isn't greatness in the kingdom. If I don't have love, I have nothing. We need to be clear about the goal of discipleship and celebrate love and its fruits.

A church full of disciples who abound in love for God and others work together in harmony. They give preference to one another. They are satisfied and are not striving or demonstrating a demanding spirit to have things their own way so they will feel better about themselves. The opposite is true of them. They are outward-focused. The love they have for God is pouring out of them and onto the world. They seek justice for the poor because of that same love. There is no shortage of money for the mission around the world. People are not trying to fill the empty void with spending and experiences that fail in their promise. They joyfully give because they love the people of the nations and can't stand the fact that they have no access to learn about the love of God. Missionary candidates are ready to go and give their lives even in the darkest places. They trust the love of God to provide their safety. There is real fellowship. Gatherings center around the love of Christ and how they are growing in this knowledge. There is open confession of sin because love of the body of Christ is safe and provides acceptance. No one is belittled for their failures or talks behind their back. Heroes are made of those who demonstrate pure love (actually Jesus is the hero). Worship is not an experience of feeling better about oneself and the songs we like but is an expression of love and adoration of a holy and loving God.

> *I believe that what we do as the church to make disciples will necessarily change if our goal is loving people. What we measure will change.*

We must have a clear vision for discipleship if we want to develop a church like that. Our hearts must be stirred for the authentic instead of the synthetic. What we celebrate will not resemble what we celebrate today. When we make a shift to the disciples who resemble the discipleship of Jesus, we join the Spirit of God and what he is doing. Only then will we see the church transformed.

Reflection Questions

1. How strong is the vision of discipleship in your ministry focused and driven by love? How can the motivation of love become more central to the mission of your ministry?

2. Based on Bernard of Clairvaux's four levels of love, where do you place yourself, and why?

    1.   Love self for your own sake.

    2.   Love God for our own sake.

    3.   Love God for his sake.

    4.   Love ourselves for God's sake.

3. If you were to use Bernard's paradigm to move people along in the depth of their love, how would you do it? How do people grow in the love that is from God?

4. Churches struggle with having enough volunteers, giving to world missions, commitment to small groups, etc. What is the approach of your ministry to address these issues, and how does the paradigm of addressing the soul take you to a different approach?

8

Am I a Loving Person?

I love you, Lord, my strength.

—Psalm 18:1

I suppose if you proposed that question to most people, they would say, "Yes, I am a loving person." I don't think the data on that kind of research project would be much different inside the church than outside the church. If people see themselves as loving people, they will have very little motivation to change. But if we ask the same people about

> *I fail every day to live out of love for others, but I am strangely not bothered enough about that to refocus my efforts on making a change in my life.*

how they see other people, they would have a very different kind of response.

I am one of those people who think they are a loving person (at least in comparison to other people). Yet I am no different than anyone else. I am not fully aware of my own failures, and I am sure others don't see me the same way I see myself. I am also sure God sees that, however, every once in a while, God gets my attention.

At a team building outing, I arranged for our entire office to attend a Met's baseball game. (Their record was terrible, so the tickets were free.) We all went, including family and even extended family. The tickets were in the nosebleed section, and other than a few other losers, we were the only ones there. We had an entire block of tickets for our group that were all together. I had given out the tickets when we left our vehicles. Everyone was laughing and enjoying themselves as we made our way to our seats. There was only one problem. When we arrived at our seats, there were people in our seats. I couldn't believe it! The whole section was empty, and people had the nerve to sit in our seats! My plans were interrupted (actually I was ticked off), so I needed to act. I went over to the elderly woman and told her she was in our seats. She started to reply that there were seats everywhere, so just take another seat. In full control, I just took another seat. No! I got angry and felt the tension throughout my entire body. I became demanding and then insisted that she move. She gave me a horrified look as she got up and moved up a few rows. What I didn't know was that the woman was my assistant's mother! Her daughter was behind me watching the entire episode play out in front of her. I was humiliated. Her view of me will never be the same.

That incident was a wake-up call for me personally to ask the question, "Am I really a loving person, or do I just act nice to some people most of the time?" What is going on in my soul? I can't tell you how many more times my soul was tempted to act that way again in the coming months, and I was stopped because I wondered whose relative that might be! I am not as loving as I think I am!

What is in the heart comes out. We can't fool everyone all the time. I was on my way to church, and I was running late. It was important for me to be on time because I was the pastor. When I got to an intersection, there was a person who was waiting to turn, but I had the right-of-way. I could have stopped and let them go, but I was in a hurry. The person in the other car honked their horn with indignation and then flipped me the bird. Out of the corner of my eye, as I was turning, I saw that it was one of my church members. And yes, she saw my face as well. We were both stunned. Awkwardness, to say the least, characterized the first couple of times we saw each other. She didn't come to church that morning (I am sure she was late for church as well as she was only one block from the church and heading in that direction). Every once in a while, we learn about our failure to love; but otherwise, we sail through life believing we are pretty good people.

Psychologists and sociologists have studied the way people see themselves. What they have universally discovered is that people see themselves in a more positive light than they see other people. In other words, they see themselves as better than others. They also see themselves better than they really are. This is true in a wide variety of areas on how they see themselves, including racism, beauty, being nice or good, ability to change, and how smart we are. We even believe our own problems are worse than anyone else's problems![14]

Cornell conducted two studies that demonstrate that people have a very high view of their own loving behavior but, in reality they are much less loving than they think. "We knew something had to be wrong when the average person thinks he or she's a better person than the average person, when the majority of Americans consider themselves to be members of an elite moral minority,"[15] says Epley, who conducted a series of revealing experiments about subjects' perception versus the reality of their moral behavior. "We wanted to know whether people feel holier than thou because they underestimate others' moral goodness, or because they overestimate their own."[16]

In the first study, people were faced with the moral dilemma of being asked how much of their fee for participating in the research study they would give to the poor (charity). They were also asked how much they thought others would contribute. At the end of the study, they were given the opportunity to donate to the poor. The result was that they predicted that they themselves would give half of their fee. They predicted that others would only give a third. In reality, when they were given the opportunity to give, they only gave a quarter!

In the second study, the researchers gave students the choice of performing an onerous, time-consuming task themselves or assigning the work to someone else. The "someone" in some cases was another college student and, in others, a

> *People are generally self-centered and will choose their own comfort over the comfort of others, as well as the fact that most people are wrong in thinking that they themselves are more likely to be altruistic.*

ten-year-old girl who presumably would have great difficulty with the task. The results were as follows: "Many students predicted they would take on the onerous task themselves, particularly when the other person was a little girl. However, most students facing an actual decision chose the easier job for themselves and were just as likely to do so whether they were assigning the difficult task to another college student or to the youngster." The fascinating takeaway from this study is that there was no difference in whether or not they were dealing with a college student or a ten-year-old little girl! The deciding factor was simply self-interest.

Self-awareness is defined by *Merriam-Webster* as a "conscious knowledge of one's own character, feelings, motives, and desires."[17] It appears that the level of self-awareness of most people is fairly low. If people have little awareness of what is driving their behavior, and even the behavior itself, the task of discipling the souls of people will be exceedingly difficult. Self-awareness must be part of the process of discipleship.

St. Augustine, in the *Confessions*, prayed, "Grant, Lord, that I may know myself that I may know Thee."[18] Here is the logic behind this statement as described by John Calvin:

> For as there exists in man something like a world of misery, and ever since we were stripped of the divine attire our naked shame discloses an immense series of disgraceful properties every man, being stung by the consciousness of his own unhappiness, in this way necessarily obtains at least some knowledge of God. Thus, our feeling of ignorance, vanity, want, weakness, in short, depravity and corruption, reminds us, (see Calvin on John 4: 10), that in the Lord, and none but He, dwell the true light of wisdom, solid virtue, exuberant goodness. We are accordingly urged by our own evil things to consider the good things of God; and, indeed, we cannot aspire to Him in earnest until we have begun to be displeased with ourselves. For what man is not disposed to rest in himself? Who, in fact, does not thus rest, so long as he is unknown to himself; that is, so long as he is contented with his own endowments, and unconscious or unmindful of his misery? Every person, therefore, on coming to the knowledge of himself, is not only urged to seek God, but is also led as by the hand to find him.[19]

Knowledge of self precedes the knowledge of the divine. It is through our understanding of our destitute state that we come to understand the marvels of the holy love of God.

John Calvin also points out that self-knowledge must be accompanied by the knowledge of God. He states, "There is no deep knowing of God without a deep knowing of self, and no deep knowing of self without a deep knowing of God."[20] It is not enough to have self-awareness. Calvin points out why:

> It is evident that man never attains to a true self-knowledge until he has previously contemplated the face of God, and come down after such

contemplation to look into himself. For (such is our innate pride) we always seem to ourselves just, and upright, and wise, and holy, until we are convinced, by clear evidence, of our injustice, vileness, folly, and impurity.[21]

The Cornell studies verify something Calvin understood centuries before. Let's not misunderstand Calvin or Augustine. They are not appealing to the need for psychologizing or getting in touch with your inner self. What they are saying is that the more we understand our inner passions and their self-centered obsession and grime, the more we will have a desire for God. The goal is not to self-actualize but to become enthralled in the beauty of God. Only then we will grasp that there is no one righteous, not even one (Rom 2:10).

> *The point is to understand what is motivating our souls. Is there something motivating our souls other than love for God and love for others? How has our soul been corrupted?*

What we are referring to when we speak of self-awareness is not the importance of understanding your personality and temperament. (There is great value in understanding that, but this is not our point at the moment.) Why do we do what we do? Could it be that we are deceived? Has Satan so blinded our eyes that we don't even know why we do what we do?

2 Corinthians 4:4 says, "The god of this age has blinded the minds of unbelievers, so that they cannot see the light of the Gospel that displays the glory of Christ, who is the image of God." Blindness is the work of the devil. He uses it to keep us in the dark. His work does not stop with unbelievers, but he is blinding believers as well. We need to see ourselves more clearly, and become more desperate to see the glory of Christ who is the image of God. Why? Because we were created to be his image bearers!

Reflection Questions

1. How do you fail to love others? Can you recall specific stories where God has revealed your need for your soul to be changed?

2. Self-awareness is key to discipleship of the soul. You can't address something that you have no knowledge. How is developing self-awareness part of your discipleship process? What has given you self-awareness?

3. What keeps people from becoming more aware of themselves? What drives their behavior on how they are perceived by others with an accurate picture of themselves?

4. In what ways can you create a discipleship process/culture that allows for and encourages self-awareness?

PART II

The Anatomy of the Soul

And now, Israel, what does the LORD *your God require of you, but to fear the* LORD *your God, to walk in all his ways, to love him, to serve the* LORD *your God with all your heart and with all your soul.*

—Deuteronomy 10:12

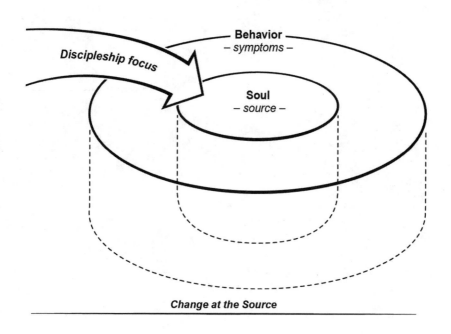

Change at the Source

9

Why Is the Soul so Crucial?

For from within, out of the heart of man, come evil thoughts,
sexual immorality, theft, murder, adultery, coveting, wickedness,
deceit, sensuality, envy, slander, pride, foolishness. All these
evil things come from within, and they defile a person.

—Mark 7:21–22

We have all had the experience of trying to help someone with their problems but with little progress. I can recall many times counseling couples who had severe marital problems that deteriorated into all-out battles. I sat before two believers who had followed Jesus longer than I was alive and who listened to thousands of sermons. They could quote Scripture (and they did to each other) and had read half the books that were in my study. Yet for some reason, they couldn't get along.

Trying to unpack the mess before me, I listened to multiple stories and accusations. While listening intently, I was trying to diagnose the exact issue or disease from which this couple suffered. The deeper we got into the stories, the more I realized that I didn't know where to begin. It reminded me of the times I took my two sons fishing, and the lines got tangled so badly there was no hope of figuring it out. It was just better to cut the line and put new line on the reel. Unfortunately, that is not an option when dealing with marriages (although that is the solution so many choose).

I was not a novice in counseling, having been a pastor for more than twenty years and possessing a degree in psychology and had studied counseling at the master's level, so I knew the presenting issues are never the real issues. So I dug deeper and deeper. I learned that the husband had post-traumatic stress disorder from his time in the service. I learned that his wife had been abused as a child. There were trust issues from patterns of lying. Financial issues complicated everything as the husband couldn't adequately provide for the family. The wife resented that she had to work ten hours a day to pay the bills. The stories of the children (who were now teens and adults) would make your hair stand on end.

My wife is very good at untangling balled-up fishing line. She has the patience and acumen for systematically working toward the goal. She won't give up (I think partly to prove to me that she can, and I can't). And sometimes, she actually salvages the line, but the fish are not caught because of the time it took to untangle the line. My experience in trying to help people with their problems leaves me wanting more. I'm not satisfied with untangling one issue only to discover another issue and another. It is clear that I am only dealing with the symptoms of deeper and bigger issues, but for some reason, we never get there.

> *Discipleship that doesn't deal with the soul is, at the very best, helpful at making people's life more manageable.*

You don't have to be a pastor in a counseling situation to recognize that trying to help other people address their issues is frustrating. Perhaps you try to help a friend who confides in you, or you are desperately attempting to rescue your child from some kind of destructive behavior. No matter what you do or say, or how much Bible you can pump into them, the results are found wanting. You wonder what is wrong. You dread situations like this because you feel so helpless.

On the one hand, it seems so simple—forgive each other and make up! Stop doing drugs! Show up on time to your place of work and bite your tongue! "Here are the three things you need to do when this arises," one might say. That must be the answer because that is what many sermons declare.

We are not stupid. We all know that there is something deeper going on inside people that is driving this sinful and destructive behavior. Instructions about how to fix it just don't work because there is something deeper fighting against the implementation of what the Bible clearly teaches. They don't want to forgive. They want to be angry. They want to be released into another marriage. No, they won't say that, but their actions betray their words. Deep down inside, there is something driving in the opposite way of Christ. This is what the Scripture calls the soul. The soul is the seat of decision-making. It is the place where motivation dwells. It is the essence of the person.

Discipleship that doesn't deal with the soul is, at the very best, helpful at making people's life more manageable. And if that is true, then perhaps it can do more harm than good because the real need in the soul is camouflaged. A managed life is not a discipled life or the life Christ intended. Preaching and teaching that helps people become more proficient at managing life so that they succeed in not dealing with their soul is counterproductive to the cause of Christ.

> *It is possible to have behavior change without soul change.*

Let me give you an example of what a managed life looks like, in contrast to a life where the soul has been transformed. A church recognizes that its members are not ordering their life in such a way that uses their finances to advance the kingdom. The exact opposite is happening. People are building bigger houses, buying newer and faster cars, taking lavish vacations, but the church has trouble caring for the church building and gives little for missions. The pastor and the elders decide that they should do some training in stewardship. They choose an off-the-shelf program that purports itself to be biblically based (not saying it isn't) and runs the program in the church. Simultaneously, the pastor decides to preach on the subject of stewardship. When the program is finished, the offerings have risen, and people seem to be saving more of their money. People are not getting over their heads in debt as often. The stewardship discipleship was a success. Right?

Well maybe it was, maybe it wasn't. We can say that it certainly was helpful to the people in the church in managing their money. There is now more money for ministry (at least for the moment). Lives look more in control and godlier because they are less flamboyant about their spending. Bible truths about spending and saving and giving were learned. What could be wrong with that?

The question I would raise is whether or not the soul was changed. It is possible to have behavior change without soul change. For instance, I have known people who went through the stewardship training for the very purpose of being more successful financially so they could have a better retirement.

Do you see the difference in the goal of soul discipleship? The goal is not a change in behavior or a managed life, but a soul transformation.

Let me give you some examples about how the soul could be addressed in relationship to money. Money in our society is often the source of our security. If the goal of the program was to make the person more financially secure (and, of course, to give ten percent or more to the church), then we did more damage to the soul. A soul that finds security in money rather than God himself is relying on an idol. The idol will be revealed at another time when the stock market crashes with only two years left before retirement, or the housing market crashes and the mortgage is underwater (even though they were good stewards in refinancing their home at a cheaper rate).

Another way money is used in our society is to demonstrate our significance. The vacations we take, the house we own, and the car we drive demonstrate that we have worth and value. Oftentimes it is a competitive game. Consciously or unconsciously, we make decisions that prop up our value in the world and community. The stewardship program may actually assist the members in being more competitive in this game. In fact, the program itself may even use prosperity as a motivator to be better steward: "If you tithe and honor God with your money, God will prosper you." I am speaking hypothetically, but the point is that we can think we are doing discipleship when, in reality, we are not addressing the soul issues, or even strengthening Satan's grip on the soul.

Before I leave this example, I want to just give some food for thought about the soul with regards to stewardship. It is important for us to recognize the difference between soul discipleship and discipleship that never gets to the soul.

A soul that is discipled in stewardship will see that everything they have is God's, and they are managers of God in using their money for the kingdom. A soul that trusts in God for security will not hoard money but be generous. A discipled soul will love those who never had access to the Gospel and give generously to missions. Like the Macedonian churches, they even give out of their extreme poverty (2 Cor 8:2). A discipled soul lives as one who is a citizen of heaven rather than one of earth. Their hope is in the future in heaven, not storing up treasures on earth (Matt. 6:19). Giving is prompted out of love for God and others, not duty or a better return on the rest of their money. To see a soul change, it takes a different approach to discipleship.

Let me be clear that I am not saying that learning biblical principles about money has no value. They have value just as learning the Ten Commandments have value. However, you can't disciple the soul with the law!

Conforming to biblical principles is no different than law keeping, especially if the soul is doing it for the wrong reasons.

In the fourth century, Basil the Great (330–79), who was the bishop of Caesarea, spoke about the role of the discipler being the "physician of the soul." He argued for the rise of disciplers who would cure the sickness of the soul rather than helping the disciples with their sickness.[22] He believed that this is only possible in the context of community rather than the current practice of monasticism, which isolated the disciple from temptation, struggle, and people. He argued that the best and only "setting in which the most important of all virtues can be formed, and that is the virtue of love."[23] His contemporary, St. Augustine, popularized this principle. Later, this idea of community to learn how to love was instituted in various settings and called the "Rule of St. Augustine." One example of this was the forming of small intimate communities by parish priests, who were called canons regular. If the goal of discipleship was love, then discipleship could not take place in the absence of community.

> I am convinced that the church is largely focusing on the symptoms of a diseased soul rather than on the root soul disease itself.
>
> If disciplers are truly the physician of the soul, they must understand and know the anatomy of the soul.

If disciplers are truly the physician of the soul, they must understand and know the anatomy of the soul. What makes the soul work? What are its motivations? How is the soul influenced? What are the sicknesses of the soul? What medicine is needed for the soul?

The critical nature of soul discipleship must be recognized and made a priority in the life of the church. The people of God are sick and needs a physician of the soul—people who understand the nature of the soul and how to treat the soul. We need to train pastors and laymen alike in the work of the soul.

The first family to come to Christ in my first church plant was very dear to me. I watched their souls come alive in the grace of Christ. This spiritual awakening was spectacular. Their passion for Christ and desire to share their love of Christ with their family and their neighbors was amazing. The husband quickly joined an evangelistic team, as he wanted to be trained to better tell the Gospel story to whoever would listen.

His wife often complained about a lower-back problem that was nagging and made her uncomfortable. She saw the doctor and had tests and X-rays, but the prescription was chiropractic in nature. Six months later, her back suddenly became unbearable. She went to the hospital, and tests revealed that she had cancer throughout her body. It was too late for treatment. She died within three weeks.

The tragedy was that for six months, the treatment that she received was not related to her problem. They were treating the symptoms rather than the disease. They didn't discover the root problem until it was too late.

I am convinced that the church is largely focusing on the symptoms of a diseased soul rather than on the root of soul disease itself. We might relieve some of the pain of the disease with biblical principles and life management technics, but underneath, the problem is strangling life.

When my middle son was sixteen, he developed a passion for cars. He dreamed of building a Pontiac Fiero (the only midengine car built in America in the '80s) that would have a supercharged three-hundred-horsepower engine. This dream led to one of the biggest projects that we would take on as a father-and-son team. We purchased a car in good shape that wasn't running and went to work. We learned so much about cars and engines along the way. Once we were ignorant, but over time, we became schooled in engine building, tuning, diagnosis, and solving problems. We made many mistakes that cost us time and money, but it was all worth it. Not only did we succeed in the build, but we became "physicians of the engine."

In the diagnosis of engine problems, you basically ask two questions: "Is this a fuel issue or spark issue?" To have successful combustion, you need both fuel and spark. The answer to this question will point you in two different directions, hopefully in the right direction. Understanding the anatomy of the engine helped us to be able to find out the proper way of solving the problem. In the same way, if we understand the anatomy of the soul, we will be able to diagnose the problem and apply the Gospel.

Our family's favorite television program at one time was House. Hugh Laurie played the part of a gifted doctor who was able to figure out the most bizarre and difficult medical issues facing the hospital. He happened to be also the most obstinate person to work with because of his stubbornness and arrogance. Sympathy is developed for Hugh's character because he himself also suffers from a debilitating disease that causes him unbearable pain. He can't heal himself even as he solves everyone else's sicknesses. All he can do to deaden his pain is to swallow a handful of pills several times a day.

The story line is somewhat predictable even though there are twists and turns along the way. The plot line is for a person with a bizarre sickness (i.e., body turning orange and then blue) and the team of doctors treat the problem unsuccessfully. Actually, the problem becomes worse from the wrong treatment over and over again until the patient almost dies. Then the brilliant doctor breaks all the rules of the hospital and medical practice and risks his career and saves the patient. He finally gets the root of the problem. Ironically, the sickness is almost always something very simple—something overlooked and simple.

That show is an allegory for the church. The disease of the soul in the church is treated in many ways with various programs, books, and teaching. But there is something missing—something basic and underlying that is causing bizarre behavior and sinful and destructive lives. Instead of identifying the underlying soul issues, the symptoms are treated with what is commonly thought to be the solutions. However, the problems continue and sometimes get worse. Until the soul is addressed, the symptoms get worse and continually manifest itself in strange ways.

Reflection Questions

1. Are you and your disciples skilled at being "physicians of the soul"?
    Are you able to diagnosis and bring solutions to the soul with spiritual
    discernment? Why or why not?

2. If the soul is the motivation and source of behavior, how can you grow
    in your wisdom and knowledge to become a physician of the soul and
    prepare others to become physicians of the soul?

3. Augustine argued that if love is the goal of discipleship, then disciple-
    ship had to be based in communities. Why are communities so neces-
    sary for disciple making when focusing on the soul?

4. How does ministry that focuses on "relieving pain" hinder discipleship
    rather than advancing discipleship? What would be a better approach?

10

The Seat of Motivation

But if from there you seek the Lord your God, you will find
him if you seek him with all your heart and with all your soul.

—Deuteronomy 4:29

We have made the assertion that the soul and the heart in Scripture are both speaking about the core of man. It is the source of all behavior. The heart and soul are used together as synonyms throughout the Scriptures. Deuteronomy 4:29 says, "But if from there you seek the Lord your God, you will find him if you seek him with all your heart and with all your soul." Joshua 22:5 instructs, "But be very careful to keep the commandment and the law that Moses the servant of the Lord gave you: to love the Lord your God, to walk in obedience to him, to keep his commands, to hold fast to him and to serve him with all your heart and with all your soul." Notice the connection of love to the soul and heart. We have not made a distinction between the two. There are many who try to define the soul more specifically and exactly, and even theologically.

The Scripture refers to the soul over eight hundred times. When writing about the soul, the Bible writers used the Hebrew word *ne'phesh* or the Greek

78   Three Passions of the Soul

word *psy·khe'*. The primary use is to refer to a life. This word can refer to animal (creature) or human life. It is not a technical term but is used generically to refer to life. Sometimes there are modifiers along with the word soul such as "eternal" or "dead."[24] The context gives us greater understanding to what is being meant by the word other than the word itself.

There are those who hold to a triune view of man. They believe that man is made up of the spirit, the soul, and the body. This is a classical Greek view of man. The Hebrew concept of man is more of a duality: body and spirit/soul. The spirit and soul are the part of man that is eternal and relates to others and God. The body is the way we relate in this world.

One verse that is often used inaccurately as a proof text about the nature of man as body, soul, and spirit is Hebrews 4:12, "For the word of God is alive and active. Sharper than any double-edged sword, it penetrates even to dividing soul and spirit, joints and marrow; it judges the thoughts and attitudes of the heart." The point is made that the word of God is able to divide the soul and spirit, so they are two entities. However, the point that is being made is not about the soul and spirit, but rather the power of the word of God. The word of God is so sharp, so powerful, so alive and active that it can divide something that is not divisible! That is the point! It is a literary devise called hyperbole (exaggeration) to make a point. You can't divide the soul and spirit any more than you can divide bones and marrow. The verse is a statement about the importance and power of the word of God, not a commentary on the anatomy of the soul (or the anatomy of the body).[25]

> It is enough to recognize that the soul/heart is important in the role of discipleship because it is the seat of what drives behavior.

It is not the purpose of this book to delve into the theological distinctions between these two positions or argue for one over the other. For our purposes, it is not relevant (interesting, but not pertinent to our discussion). You can hold to either position and still track with where we are going in understanding the soul. It is enough to recognize that the soul/heart is important in the role of discipleship because it is the seat of what drives behavior. This is why God spoke through Ezekiel, prophesying the need for a new heart. Jesus taught us that out of the heart comes every good or evil thing (Matt. 15:19).

The key issue for our discussion about the soul/heart as it relates to discipleship is that the soul is the target of the deep work of the Holy Spirit.

Discipleship is not about the symptoms of our sin disease but about the cure of the source of our sin. That source is the soul/heart.

The sickness of our soul is that it is controlled by the power of sin rather than that of the Spirit. Romans 8:1–8 teaches us that Christ came to deal with this soul problem:

> There is therefore now no condemnation for those who are in Christ Jesus. For the law of the Spirit of life has set you free in Christ Jesus from the law of sin and death. For God has done what the law, weakened by the flesh, could not do. By sending his own Son in the likeness of sinful flesh and for sin, he condemned sin in the flesh, in order that the righteous requirement of the law might be fulfilled in us, who walk not according to the flesh but according to the Spirit. For those who live according to the flesh set their minds on the things of the flesh, but those who live according to the Spirit set their minds on the things of the Spirit. For to set the mind on the flesh is death, but to set the mind on the Spirit is life and peace. For the mind that is set on the flesh is hostile to God, for it does not submit to God's law; indeed, it cannot. Those who are in the flesh cannot please God.

Jesus came to deal with our soul problem. The soul, which was made in the image of God, reflecting God in the creation through perfect love, was destroyed when sin entered it. The soul then became powerless to be the image bearer it was created to be. Christ came and gave us his life-giving Spirit and freed us from the bondage of a sinful soul. Christ has freed us. We are free indeed!

Nelson Mandela was imprisoned in South Africa for opposing the evil crime of apartheid that was perpetrated on the majority of South Africans who were black. He was released in 1990 after spending twenty-seven years in prison. The newly elected South African president, F. W. de Klerk began working to end apartheid. Together, de Klerk and Nelson Mandela accepted the Nobel Peace Prize for ending the hateful and demeaning practice of systematic discrimination by race. In Mandela's speech, he makes it clear that there is a difference in being "set free" and "living free." The law had been changed, but it would take years and even decades before those who were set free actually were living free.[26]

In the same way, we are set free from the law of sin and death by the cross. Yet our soul's propensity toward sin, rather than following the Spirit, which is

> *There is a difference in being set free and living free.*

availed to us, must be overcome. Sin is defeated. It doesn't have control. Yet we must yield to the life-giving Spirit made available to us. We are not under obligation to do what the sinful nature urges us to do. The power of the Spirit is ours. The power of sin has been broken.

Paul reveals his own battle in a very personal way. We are free, but we struggle to live free from sin. Romans 7:14–17 says:

> So the trouble is not with the law, for it is spiritual and good. The trouble is with me, for I am all too human, a slave to sin. I don't really understand myself, for I want to do what is right, but I don't do it. Instead, I do what I hate. But if I know that what I am doing is wrong, this shows that I agree that the law is good. So I am not the one doing wrong it is sin living in me that does it. (NLT)

The battle is for the soul. The soul is already rescued. Christ did that, and it is complete. The Spirit is given to bring about life—a life in the Spirit. But the soul is in need of transformation. But notice that the transformation is not by the law; it is by the Spirit. If we can understand the nature of the sinful soul, perhaps that will also help us to understand the means of the freedom that is ours in the Spirit.

Reflection Questions

1. Our sinful nature has corrupted our souls, so we struggle with living out of love for God. The struggle is real. How have you understood this struggle, and how have you overcome the struggle or helped others overcome their struggle?

2. Has your approach been inside-the-cup or outside-the-cup help? Explain.

3. Paul says the things he wants to do he doesn't do. Why? The soul desires that what is contrary to the Spirit. How does this relate to the three passions of the soul (acceptance, significance, and security)?

4. Can you identify with Mandela's speech when he differentiates between "being free" and "living free"? Why or why not?

11

The Sinful Soul

*For the desires of the flesh are against the Spirit, and the desires
of the Spirit are against the flesh, for these are opposed to each
other, to keep you from doing the things you want to do.*

—Galatians 5:17

The soul of man was created to be an image bearer of God. We have
learned from Scripture that the primary focus of that image bearing is to
reflect the love of God. We are created to love God and love others. Every
law and directive in Scripture is fulfilled when we bear that image. However,
the image of God in man was marred by sin. The Scripture has a lot to say
about the result of sin on our souls.

The Greek word that is translated "flesh" is *sarx*. The Scripture speaks of
the flesh personified as if it is a person within you. The personification of evil
is a literary device to teach that our own nature has desires and passions that
are contrary to the Spirit of God ("the sinful nature wants to do evil" [Gal
5:17]). The flesh is not a literal person inside of you. In the same chapter,
there is a list of the deeds of the flesh: "sexual immorality, impurity, lustful
pleasures, idolatry, sorcery, hostility, quarreling, jealousy, outbursts of anger,
selfish ambition, dissension, division, envy, drunkenness, wild parties, and
other sins like these" (Gal 5:19–21). Ephesians 2:3 indicates that craving for
evil is universal and that even the mind has been corrupted. The depravity

extends to our reason and thoughts. Jeremiah 17:9 states it like this, "The heart is deceitful above all things, and desperately sick; who can understand it?" The soul is corrupted in such a way that it is beyond reason and makes little sense. It is confused and is confusing when we see it in action. The soul is sick.

1 John 3:4 and Romans 8:5–9 describe the soul as lawless. The soul's condition is desperate for the Spirit because it can't change itself. It can't obey the law. It can't love. Its passions are not for loving God or others. Its passion is for oneself apart from the love of God.

The amazing Gospel story is that God so loved these depraved souls that he sent his only Son as an atoning sacrifice (1 John 4:10). He also gave us his Spirit as proof that we live in him and he in us. We are born again and made new. We are not renovated but regenerated. There is hope for our souls. That hope is found in Christ Jesus alone.

The Scriptural evidence is clear that our entire being is corrupted by sin. Our soul's destruction involves our strength (will), the mind, and the heart. The Spirit of God is given to us as the remedy for the regenerated soul. Titus 3:4–6 declares, "But when God our Savior revealed his kindness and love, he saved us, not because of the righteous things we had done, but because of his mercy. He washed away our sins, giving us a new birth and new life through the Holy Spirit. He generously poured out the Spirit upon us through Jesus Christ our Savior" (NLT).

The personification of the flesh is a very real thing. We know him well. At times, he surprises us, and we give into his sway. You could be on a church retreat in the middle of the gorgeous snow-capped mountains experiencing incredible and insightful teaching for the Word when you glance down at your phone, and there is a text message from someone you don't know. At the break, you take a peek and open the e-mail only to discover an invitation to view some pictures. You know you shouldn't click the link, but you do anyway. In a moment, you are transferred from the top of the spiritual mountain to the valley of destruction.

How does that happen? Why are we so susceptible to the attacks of Satan and the flesh? What is going on in our soul? There is an answer to that question. You can understand your soul, at least to a greater degree than you do now. There is hope. You can live a life of holiness, but God must first deal with your soul.

The Scripture warns us that we should be aware of the devil's schemes (Eph 6:13). 1 Peter 5:8 warns us that "your enemy the devil prowls around like a roaring lion looking for someone to devour." We need to be alert and aware of what he is up to. Do you know your weakness? Do you know how to stand your ground against the devil? There are underlying issues in the soul that make us susceptible to the devil's scheme and to our weak flesh.

If we are to disciple people, we must understand the *where* and *how* Satan attacks. I am not talking about the sending of a seductive e-mail invitation, but I am speaking about what in our soul attracts you to investigate that which you know will destroy your soul. There are few people who understand what is happening and why they keep falling. The giving of more Scriptures to memorize will not fix it. Making a promise, even to an accountability partner, will not protect you. You and I both know you will lie about it when you are asked. You must discover that which is attracting you to that e-mail and attack it at its roots.

Understanding the three passions of the soul and how they work to drive your thinking, attractions, feelings, and actions are necessary. It is urgent. Until we refocus our ministry to one another in a way that gets to the root of our failures, we will continue in destructive pathways.

The power of temptation is that it has appeal to your soul. Jesus was tempted in every way just like us, and yet was able not to sin (Heb 4:15). He was able to throw off the temptation because there was nothing in him that was attracted to sin. What attracts us to sin? Our souls are sick. They have been corrupted. But there is hope because we are not under the power of sin any longer. We are not bound. Sin is not our destiny. Christ has rescued us and set us free. We are free indeed.

The road to freedom has already been made for us. Discipleship is the process of living in that freedom. As we grow in discipleship, we will experience greater freedom to love like Christ. We are sanctified by the grace of God through the work of Christ on the cross. But God is sanctifying us by his Spirit daily. Soul discipleship, when understood, will help in this process, because it reveals the deformation of our soul and the Gospel can be applied.

Reflection Questions

1. Christ was tempted in every way like we are but was able not to sin. What was it about Jesus that he did not respond to temptation as we do?

2. Can you put words or specific reasons for your attraction to sin and temptation? Are you aware of what is driving your soul to respond to temptation?

3. Identify a temptation or sin that you recently succumbed. Ask God to show you what was in your soul that attracted you to that sin.

12

Three Passions
of the Soul

Beloved, I urge you as sojourners and exiles to abstain from
the passions of the flesh, which wage war against your soul.

—1 Peter 2:11

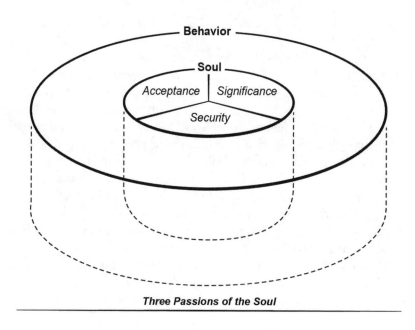

Three Passions of the Soul

As a student of psychology as well as theology, I was fascinated by how natural science has studied man—the soul. Modern psychology is demonstratively humanistic, atheistic, and naturalistic in philosophy, yet we can learn something from what they perceive. Psychology theorizes why man does what he does. Here is its question: "How can we explain human behavior?" The answer to that question is varied and divided. Human beings are not always predictable, making the study of human behavior a mystery to be studied. Theories abound.

It is not my purpose to review every theory of psychology and human personality. Each theory does add some understanding to our knowledge of human behavior and can even help us to understand what is going on in the soul. Some are more helpful than others.

Personality theories have been developed around traits, types, psychoanalytic, behaviorist, humanistic, social cognitive, genetics, and evolutionary theories. For example, those who follow a Darwinian approach study human behavior and try to explain it through the theory of the evolution of the species and natural selection. The theory states that human behavior can be explained by the desire of man to survive. Genetic theorists are busy trying to understand and predict human behavior simply on biology and genetic history. The Human Genome Project gave space for this kind of study. The theory is trying to understand how

> *What he discovered was that each individual could be understood, and relationships could be improved once one understood what was motivating themselves and others to achieve self-worth.*

small changes in DNA determine behavior. Most people are familiar with psychoanalytic theories like that of Freud, which have built theories of behavior around how we respond to childhood experiences and how they shape our world. These theories have had some impact in understanding human behavior, but largely have been discredited and have demonstrated little help to understanding the complexity of human behavior.

One theory that has challenged me to think much more deeply about the issues of the soul comes from a psychologist named Elias Porter. He was a peer of Carl Rogers, Thomas Gordon, and Abraham Maslow. He worked first at Ohio State University and then at the University of Chicago. His primary contribution was in the area of relationship awareness theory and psychometric testing. He was a practical psychologist in that his work was not merely theoretical, but he applied his theories to develop practical helps to the world of government and business. His work is still used extensively in these arenas.[27]

He was influenced by Carl Rogers while he was one of his students. Carl Rogers theorized that behavior was influenced and directed by the goal of self-actualization. His theory would fall into the category of humanistic psychology. Clearly, Rogers's belief that man was seeking self-fulfillment or self-actualization drove Elias Porter's research.

Porter began to research what was driving man (soul) to have self-worth. *Self-worth* was the term he chose to describe the driving force of the soul. Self-worth is what made the person feel good and satisfied. His theory explored different ways that people were motivated to achieve self-worth. He experimented with many kinds of motivational drives and eventually settled on three major motivations people have to achieve self-worth. The three ways are through altruistic behavior and care, assertive-directing, and analytic-anonymizing. Those are technical terms that he chose to use. For the sake of simplifying his theory, the three motivations are caring, winning, and being accurate or right. He believed that every person is a unique combination of these three motivational drives to achieve self-worth for themselves.[28]

His theory has a second component. He believed that people chose behaviors directed by motivational drives, which he called their MVS (Motivational Value System).

> *What he observed is that man is passionately pursuing his own self-worth. He is seeking to make his mark. He is motivated first and primarily to feel good about oneself.*

The combinations of these three motivational drives were arranged into seven major MVS types. His research discovered that by testing for these three motivational drives through a psychometric instrument, he could better understand them and why they made the behavior choices that they made. In other words, what he discovered was that each individual could be understood, and relationships could be improved once one understood what was motivating oneself and others to achieve self-worth. We have titled these drives the three passions of the soul.

Porter's theory has been around for more than forty years and has been used in the government and business world to help people work better together and more effectively. The psychometric tools that he developed have a high degree of reliability (get the same result each time) and have a high-face validity (those who take the assessment believe the results describe them and their motivations accurately).

What was it that Porter discovered that is so valuable to the business world that they will seek training and consultants, as well as spend millions of dollars to learn? I believe that Porter stumbled on something greater than he realized at the time of his death. I believe that Porter had discovered and labeled the anatomy of the soul. The soul is the place of decision and behavior. He was able to successfully identify the motivational drives of the soul and why people do what they do.

The Hebrew word that translated *soul* is similar to the Hebrew word for neck. The etymology of the word *soul* appears to be related to the neck. The neck directs the focus of the person. The head is turned by the neck. The soul is like that. It directs the focus, attention, direction, and behavior of life.[29]

> **When the soul is focused on achieving worth for itself, it has no boundaries. It will trample on others whenever necessary to achieve its goal.**

I have included a graphic of the descriptors for each motivational value system (combination of the three motivational drives) in the Appendix so you can better understand the detail of the tool. You can learn more about the SDI and Porter's theory, as well as the training tools from TOTALSDI.COM or from CHANGED2LEAD.COM. The purpose of this chapter is not to educate you fully on his theories or make you an expert on the SDI, but to relate his theory and learning to the anatomy of the soul. I found the SDI assessment as a helpful tool in diagnosing the soul's passion and how one pursues worth apart from God. For this reason, I have begun to refer to the SDI (Strength Deployment Inventory) as the "soul diagnostic instrument."

Let us start by relating his theory of human behavior to the soul by examining his theory that man desires to achieve self-worth. Some might object right away because the Bible teaches that man's chief end is to worship God and enjoy him forever—love God (*Westminster Shorter Catechism*). I would agree. However, Porter was observing what people are *actually* doing and what drives their behavior, not what we *should* be doing. What he observed is that man is passionately pursuing his own self-worth. He is seeking to make his mark. He is motivated first and primarily to feel good about oneself. I find his observation hard to argue against.

The Scripture concurs with this analysis. Man is self-centered, not others-centered or God- centered. Philippians 2:4 says, "Let each of you look not only to his own interests, but also to the interests of others." Natural man is interested in himself and the change in discipleship that needs to take place is to be interested in the needs of others. 1 John 3:17 challenges this self-love: "But if anyone has the world's goods and sees his brother in need, yet closes his heart against him, how does God's love abide in him?" (ESV).

We don't have to instruct the soul to love itself. That is the fleshly soul's bent. Only when God's love abides in man does he place the needs of others above himself. 2 Timothy 3:2–4 leaves no doubt about the fleshly soul when it says, "For people will be lovers of self, lovers of money, proud, arrogant, abusive, disobedient to their parents, ungrateful, unholy, heartless, unappeasable, slanderous, without self-control, brutal, not loving good, treacherous, reckless, swollen with conceit, lovers of pleasure rather than lovers of God..." When the soul is focused on achieving worth for itself, it has no boundaries. It will trample on others whenever necessary to achieve its goal.

James 4:1–2 gives us a glimpse into the unregenerate soul, "What causes quarrels and what causes fights among you? Is it not this, that your passions are at war within you? You desire and do not have, so you murder. You covet and cannot obtain, so you fight and quarrel." What we are most passionate about is ourselves. According to Porter and his research, the best explanation of human behavior is that man is passionate about himself and feeling good about himself. His study shows that we do this in different ways, but the goal is the same.

But let us not be too quick to judge man or we may quickly be judging ourselves. Look more closely at what it means to achieve self-worth. Another way to describe self-worth would be self-love. Up until this point in the book, we have not defined love in any detail. What we have said is that love is defined by Scripture through the example of Christ: "This is love, that God sent his only son into the world to make atonement for our sins" (1 John 4:9). John also described love when he quoted Jesus, who said, "This is my commandment: Love each other in the same way I have loved you. There is no greater love than to lay down one's life for one's friends" (John 15:12–13). Love is a selfless act of putting the needs of others before your own needs. As described by Christ, it is sacrificing for the sake of others.

As I learned more about the theory of Porter and used the SDI psychometric instrument to measure my own MVS, I realized that I am very predictable in how I act toward others in achieving my self-worth. That was disturbing to me at one level because what it meant was that I was being controlled at some level by my desire to feel good about myself. To put it more harshly and bluntly, I was being controlled at some level by my own passion for myself. I love myself! I've been a follower of Jesus for more than forty years. I consider myself a sold-out disciple of Christ. But what I was beginning to digest is that my behavior has much more "flesh" in it than I ever thought.

What was even more disturbing to me is that all the discipling that I have had over forty years did not move the needle much in the area of self-love. My motivation in life that predicts my behavior most successfully is that of self-worth and a desire to feel good about myself. I am sure that I heard many sermons and taught many sermons on loving others. I had godly mentors who modeled for me what it meant to love others. I taught sermon series and Bible studies on 1 Corinthians 13 but without much impact. I don't want to be too harsh on myself or others. Maybe what could be said is that I learned to temper my behavior that my internal drive was still driving me toward.

> **What was even more disturbing to me is that all the discipling that I have had over forty years did not move the needle much in the area of self-love.**

What I began to wonder about is whether or not discipleship might be more effective if it revealed and addressed the motivation of the heart/soul. In a rather short period of time, I became aware of my own motivations and drives and how they controlled me. That journey has transformed how I live, how I pursue Christ, and how I disciple people.

Is Self-Worth Wrong?

I want to challenge us to think deeper about the concept of self-worth. Porter and others who work in the field of psychology would not attach any negativity to the word *self-worth*. They would see it as something healthy and necessary for human beings to possess. In the Christian world, the concept is extremely negative. The concept is attached to self-love, which is not compatible with love for God and for others. Or is it?

If we don't answer this question sufficiently and adequately, we will get lost before we proceed deeper in the understanding of the soul. The confusion about the concept of self-worth has been a source of contention in the church as it relates to Christian counseling. I realize that Christian counseling has a broad spectrum, but clearly, there is tension around the biblical nature of self-worth.

Recently, I was coaching a young pastor when he mentioned to me that he has nixed some worship songs they had been singing as a congregation. When I asked to give an example, he mentioned a song that had the words, "I am no longer a slave, but a child of God." I was curious, so I probed more deeply on how that was offensive. His response was thoughtful and theological. He simply explained that our culture is so focused on *me* and being loved, that he didn't want to feed the insatiable desire to be loved by singing songs that glorified me over God. I found this conversation fascinating, especially in light of the fact that this was a song us-

> "Do nothing from selfish ambition or conceit, but in humility count others more significant than yourselves" (Philippians 2:3).

ing words quoted directly from Paul's letter to the Romans. In some circles of the church, we are so consumed with breaking the culture of me that we are afraid to sing songs that teach us about God's love for us as a child of God. I reminded him that "God so loved the world that he gave…" We are the objects of God's love, and this is a huge piece of the Gospel we proclaim.

I have trained hundreds of people to train other people in the use of SDI assessments, which measure how people achieve self-worth. The question always is raised on whether or not the concept is biblical or if we should even be discussing the topic. Self-worth, when misunderstood is a problem for many. Too much baggage comes along with it. It is worth our time to delve deeper into this concept as I believe it will unlock more of what is going on in the soul.

There is no doubt that the Scriptures articulate that self-love is the source and enemy of loving our neighbor. Philippians 2:21 articulates this bluntly, "For they all seek their own interests, not those of Jesus Christ." Self-love is linked to self-seeking: "But those who are self-seeking and do not obey the truth, but obey unrighteousness, there will be wrath and fury" (Rom 2:8).

But let's explore the soul prior to the Fall. We need to remember that God created the world and all that it is, it including human souls. He distinguished the human souls from every other form of life by breathing life into them. He made them in his own image so they could be image bearers, demonstrating

God's love in the kingdom on earth. God walked amongst them, and they related together in peace and joy. In summary, love existed between the Trinity and human souls. God declared this was very good.

Yes!

If all this is true, what is the worth of man? Prior to the Fall, should Adam and Eve have had self-worth? Certainly, God gave them their worth and saw their worth. Is it appropriate for Adam and Eve to acknowledge their worth? I believe it is. But we must acknowledge the source of their worth. The source of their worth was God himself. They did not need to earn their worth. They couldn't become greater in their worth. It was a gift they received from God. They received their worth from their Creator. So we can at least say that prior to the Fall, man had worth. Self-worth on the part of human souls was appropriate. We might even say if they didn't have self-worth, they were condemning the very thing God said was very good! If they despised themselves, they would have rejected God, for they were made in his image to be image bearers. What gave them worth was that they were image bearers.

> Self-worth on the part of human souls was appropriate. We might even say if they didn't have self-worth, they were condemning the very thing God said was very good.

Now let's move to the Fall and the consequences of sin in the souls of men. We know that the image of God was marred, for they no longer were reflecting the image of God to the world, which was their design and purpose. The consequence of the Fall quickly led to every kind of sin to the point that the Creator chose to flood the earth and destroy the greatness of sin. After the Fall, did man lose his self-worth? Can man look at his soul and declare his self-worth as a created soul after the Fall? This is a critical and important question.

My answer to that question is yes. The human soul is still created in the image of God, even though he does not reflect that image, as was his purpose. The worth of the human soul was not lost in the Fall. In fact, God so loved the world that he sent his one and only Son into the world to die and redeem those souls. If the soul did not have worth, then why did God so....love? By that statement, I am not saying that the souls are lovely. But it is God's love that makes us worth something.

Here is the key to breaking through the confusion about self-worth. What we really are objecting to when we hear the word *self-worth* is that somehow the human soul has created his own worth. The Scriptures are clear that the human soul is corrupt, and it can't please God. It is bent upon evil.

The very nature of the Fall is instructive. Adam and Eve were tempted to eat of the forbidden tree because they were seeking something they thought they wanted/needed apart from God. They were seeking something to add to their worth. That kind of self-worth must be rejected, as it is the foundational sin. It rejects the source of our worth who is God himself. I believe Porter is right. Man seeks self-worth through his behavior. It is the driving force of his life. It is the best explanation of why people do what they do.

The key to understanding self-worth is to understand the source. If the source is God himself, the creator of the Universe, then yes, self-worth is biblical and in its proper place. If the source of self-worth is anywhere else than with the Creator, then our self-worth produces pride and arrogance.

The key to understanding self-worth is to understand the source. If the source is God himself, the creator of the Universe, then yes, self-worth is biblical and in its proper place. If the source of self-worth is anywhere else than with the Creator, then our self-worth produces pride and arrogance or disappointment. What is worse is that all our behaviors and relationships are designed with the purpose of increasing our self-worth. Oftentimes, our pursuit of self-worth is at the expense of others.

Self-worth is something that is given to us as a gift from God, not something that can be earned and developed. Attempts at striving after self-worth results in selfishness and, ultimately, broken relationships. Love for others can't compete with unbridled pursuit of self-love. We are image bearers, not image creators!

Reflection Questions

1. Porter's theory of personality states that people are driven by the desire for self-worth. If his theory is correct, what implications do you see for making disciples of Jesus?

2. Do you think most people are aware that they are driven in their behavior to achieve self-worth? Can you identify your own behavior and how you achieve self-worth?

3. How do you define love? What do you think of the definition of the author (putting the needs of others before your own, following the example of Christ)?

4. How important is it in discipling others that people know what is driving their self-worth and pursuit of self-worth?

5. As a physician of the soul, how can you learn to discern what is driving self-worth?

13

The Soul's Pursuit of Worth

They replied, "Let one of us sit at your right and the other at your left in your glory."

—Mark 10:37

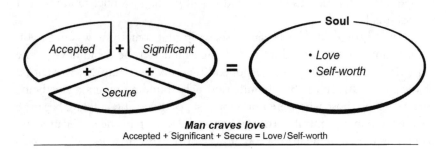

Man craves love
Accepted + Significant + Secure = Love / Self-worth

The soul's pursuit of worth is the driving force of behavior. Since the Fall, there has been a void that needs to be filled. God never stopped loving, but man's sin separated himself from that love. That void or hole is so large that it cannot be adequately filled by anything we can do. However, that does not stop us from passionately pursuing the goal. It appears that for a time, the things we do seem to fill back the hole for a time, but before long, the hole begins to sink further down. This pursuing self-worth is exhausting and all-consuming.

Let me give you one example of this all-consuming passion that leads eventually to self-destruction. The example I am choosing to share is not that of a non-Christian but one of a pastor. I have chosen this example to demonstrate that a seminary degree and "successful" ministry does not exclude any of us from sin's peril.

A young man who was saved out of a family of alcoholism and debauchery had his life turned inside out by the Gospel of Jesus Christ. He abandoned everything to serve his savior. After graduation from seminary and being mentored by one of the leading pastors/writers in the evangelical world for a year, he was called to plant a church. After a difficult period of several years, the church began to bear tremendous fruit. People were being saved, healed, and freed from their addictions. It was a church that was written about in prayer journals and celebrated by those who watched at a distance. The places they had been meeting were no longer able to house the ministry, so a large building program was begun. This building would dwarf any church in the area and be in a prominent location. By the time the building was completed and a dedication service was held, the church had imploded.

What happened? How could such a fruitful ministry be cut so short? The answer to that question is complex, but at the center of the collapse was a failure to disciple the heart of the pastor from the time of his conversion. He did not lack in the area of visionary leadership, ability to preach, or passion for the lost. What he was missing and is still missing is understanding what was driving his soul.

At first, little evidences began to show up that something was not right. A large donor was attacked for not giving as much as he could have to the building fund. A family that questioned his approach to ministry was cut off at the knees through public humiliation. The building program was being threatened by those who were not seen as supportive. The building began to be more and more central to the mission as the hole in his heart began to expand. He needed more affirmation of his worth. Anyone who spoke into his life was dismissed and seen as an enemy. Those who were close to him didn't know what to do as they didn't recognize the pastor who was now leading them. Many attempts to rescue him were made by those who loved him, but to no avail. Eventually he was dismissed unanimously by his board in great sadness. Hundreds of people were despondent and destroyed. The reputation of Christ was tarnished. The community that once saw the church as a place of rescue and love was now looked upon with suspicion.

I tell this story because it is not unique. One can only fill the hole so long before it demands more than anyone can give. This pastor was using his ministry to achieve self-worth. This pastor used his ministry, but others use their spouse. Others their children. Some their work. The alternatives are numerous.

Porter identified three motivations to achieve self-worth. We are a combination of all three, but our behavior

> When someone's self-worth is threatened, it causes conflict. Conflict often results in a demanding spirit. A demanding spirit is a soul that is striving for self-worth at the expense of loving others.

is influenced more by the most prominent motivation. For this pastor, his dominant motivation was winning or having significance. Those who seek self-worth through significance use achievement, advancement, movement, winning, and directing resources to achieve their goal. This pastor was filling his hole by reaching people with the Gospel! Yes. We can even use good things to achieve self-worth in ways God never intended. When his success was threatened, the hole began to expand and he became more desperate.

When someone's self-worth is threatened, it causes conflict. Conflict often results in a demanding spirit. A demanding spirit is a soul that is striving for self-worth at the expense of loving others. The soul must have something that it desperately needs. We can even have a demanding spirit with God himself. Sometimes you will hear this in the way people pray. There is a sense of desperation with a demanding spirit because the hole is expanding, and nothing seems to fill it.

Ministry was never given to us to achieve self-worth. When it is used to gain self-worth, it becomes extremely dangerous. Actually, anything that is used to achieve self-worth can become destructive. If we use money to achieve self-worth, anything that threatens our financial gain will create severe conflict. Even a beautiful wife can be used as way to achieve self-worth.

When self-worth is the goal, we will practically do anything and everything to not lose. What we never thought we do, we end up doing because there is no other option other than lose all my worth. I have seen pastors who give up all their integrity to retain self-worth. They lie and destroy people's lives.

> **When self-worth is the goal, we will practically do anything and everything to not lose.**

There are two ways to gain self-worth. We can get it from God and our adoption as sons of God, or we can get it from striving after it through substitutes. The Gospel offers the fullness of God's love. It is graciously given. It is free. It is a gift. That love transforms the soul through the Spirit of the living God. The Spirit is the agent of change, as we will soon explore. But the other way of filling the need for love is to strive after it apart from God. Our behaviors are shaped by this striving.

We should also note that we are all unique although we are made in the image of God and are created to be image bearers. It is God who forms us (Jer 1:5). He knows us in our inner being— soul. He creates us the way he wants us to be for his purposes. We are different and unique with personality. 1 Corinthians 12–14 teaches us that we should not try to be something we are not. God gifts us according to his Spirit and his will. Noses will never serve as feet! They are designed for different purposes, but all the parts of the body are put together to accomplish the purposes of God.

It is important to recognize these truths because discipleship does not have the purpose of making us all the same. God's imprint on each of us is unique and should be celebrated. God does not love one more than another because of their uniqueness. We are all loved…are significant to him, accepted by him, and secure in him. This is a wonderful and beautiful truth. It is the foundation and outflow of the Gospel.

Let me introduce this concept from another angle. Each of us gets pleasure from contributing to the whole but in different ways. Different things feel good to each of us in particular. The things that I enjoy doing and feeling a sense of joy from are very different from my wife.

My wife loves to help people from behind the scene. She doesn't want to be up-front. She is content and even happy to simply know that she has contributed to help someone or something succeed by supporting their efforts. She loves organizing things! I don't get it. She loves things put in the "right" order. She spends hours reorganizing closets and dishes and draws and feels a sense of satisfaction when she is done.

The very last thing I want to do with my time is organize my closet! I am just fine with the clothes thrown on the chair. And I am not good at organizing, so nobody wants me to help them from behind the scenes to do that. If I organized a retreat, it would be missing half of what is needed, and it is just possible that I booked the wrong dates! But if you ask me to come up with the topic of the retreat and speak, or drive the focus and direct a team to a goal, I'm your guy.

We get joy and satisfaction from very different things. Our souls are wired differently. In the case of my wife, very complimentary. That wiring is from God and for God. When I do what God has created for me to do, I feel a sense of fulfillment. It is motivating to contribute in your strengths. That is God's design. Together we are the body. But what if we use our strengths to get self-worth instead of using it for God's glory and his purposes? What if we take what God has given us for his glory and use it for our glory? That is exactly what we do when our soul is not full of the love of God. Our empty souls demand love because that is what we were created for. Because we don't know and experience the love of God in all of its fullness as given to us in the Gospel, we live in such a way to achieve it in other ways.

The example given above about the pastor who planted a large church but imploded is an example of a person wired by God to lead people, give direction, and achieve great things for the kingdom. Instead, he used his wiring to build his significance. When things didn't go as he needed or demanded, he began to abuse God's people. The hole in his heart could never be filled by his achievements or importance, so his soul became more demanding. Contrast this story with the apostle Paul who had a similar wiring. He was an achiever of all achievers. Whatever he put his mind to, he was able to accomplish. He was direct, forceful, goal-oriented, focused, and overcame every obstacle. The difference was that Paul understood his identity in Christ. More than seventy times, Paul referred to being "in Christ" in

> *Because we don't know and experience the love of God in all of its fullness as given to us in the gospel, we live in such a way to achieve it in other ways.*

his biblical writings. He cherished his sonship. His need for significance was met by the love of God expressed to him through the atoning sacrifice of Christ. He didn't need to prove anything. His service was not for himself but for the King of kings.

In the next section, we will talk about the redemption of our souls and how, through discipleship, the significant motivation is powerful for the kingdom. But when the significant part of the soul is engaged for self-worth, it has great potential to destroy. It runs over people, it is demanding, it is unrelenting and even scary. It gets loud and overbearing. This persona (the outward manifestation of our inward reality) is not that difficult to recognize. It carries itself with confidence and is bold. Gestures are usually large. Communication is direct and in bullet points for efficiency because they are in a hurry to get more done. Impatience is another clue. They are always talking vision and what is coming next. Change is almost always the solution to every problem. Only when the soul comes to be controlled by the Holy Spirit, and the fleshly need for self-worth is met in our sonship, is God's design for how he wired us useful to his kingdom.

God has designed some to contribute to the kingdom through caring and altruism. They are motivated by helping people belong and being cared for. They have antennas on their heads that detect when someone is hurting, being left out, or will be adversely affected by some decision or event. If they hear the word *help*, they are quick to act and meet the need. You know these people. They are fun loving and just love being with people.

When they are full of the love of God and are walking in the Spirit, they are the hands and feet of Christ ministering to the neediest amongst us. They are compassionate and don't hesitate to sacrifice for the sake of others.

Remaining and abiding is all about the love of God.

If the soul is wired this way but is not walking in the Spirit and experiencing the fullness of God's love, this same person can become a person who needs to be needed. When I was a newbie youth pastor, I met such a person. She was the most compassionate person in the church, always serving and available. My first impression was that this was an amazing woman and an example to the rest of the flock. That did not last too long. A leadership team was formed and made a decision which she believed was going to hurt a particular person—someone close to her. Suddenly, the caring demeanor was turned into anger and passive aggression. I remember asking the question, "How could such a caring person be so destructive to so many people?" The answer is that she was using her wiring to build up her own self-worth rather than doing it for the kingdom. It wasn't revealed until this event occurred.

Self-sacrifice can look godly, but it also can be a way of earning the love of others. When the new structure no longer required self-sacrifice, she became demanding to the point where she wouldn't talk to anyone and eventually left the church, along with her confused husband. It was clear to me when speaking to him that this wasn't the first time this happened. He preferred to go with his wife and preserve the peace in the household rather than address the hole in his wife's heart.

The apostle John was wired to help others. He talks more than any other writer about the love of God and acceptance. He was motivated to take care especially the needy and to make sure they had a place at the table and belonged. He used that motivation for the kingdom because he was nourished by the love of God. His famous and life-shaping teaching in John 15 about abiding in the vine demonstrates to me that he knew the secret of discipleship. He summarizes his illustration about abiding in verse 9: "Remain in my love."

Remaining and abiding is all about the love of God. John knew he was fully accepted and that he belonged in the family of God. It is no coincidence that John ends his Gospel with the story of Peter being accepted by Christ after he had denied him three times. This moving story of Christ's affirmation of Peter given three times for the three times he failed demonstrates John's focus on how the Gospel causes us to be fully accepted and belong to God. His son, Jesus, made this possible, and it does change us. We don't have to extract love from others by being helpful or caring, but we can use our wiring for the kingdom and do it out of the love for the Father rather than self-love.

God has also designed some souls to be wired to express the love of God through using their lives to bring safety and security. They are motivated by making sure things are done in the right way. They are champions of justice and want to make sure that all people are safe. They think deeply about these things and analyze facts, situations, and structures to make sure nothing is missed. They pay attention to detail that others miss.

Personally, I have little motivation in my soul for security, so it is the most difficult for me to understand. However, my father was wired this way, and my wife has a strong security component. As one with little security in my wiring, I can aggravate my wife quite easily. I tend to be riskier in decisions and don't analyze things very long or in much detail, causing her much angst.

Those whose souls are wired for security as a primary motivation also reflect the image of God. God is a God of order and knowledge. He set the *Green* world in place with mathematic formulas and is intricate in his designs (Ps 147:4). He numbers the hair on our heads (Luke 12:7).

These souls are not difficult to recognize. They are most comfortable when alone and often look uncomfortable in public places. They use few gestures when speaking, and when they do, they are small and understated. Their speech is measured and efficient. They are not too emotional and are factual.

Souls with a wiring for security can also use their strengths to achieve self-worth. I worked with someone wired for security on a church-planting team once. He was well-read and researched. He had an answer for any question that arose. He was great at writing discipleship material and volunteered readily to contribute. He contributed to the team in a way that no one else on the team was able.

He served on the leadership team for three years. During that time, there were ups and downs. While he was contributing heavily to the team and church plant, he also caused much conflict. He often pushed his knowledge and was rigid in his approach to things. When the team chose a direction, and the direction was different than the "right" way in his mind, he would disengage. He often said things in public gatherings that were interpreted by others as insensitive and hurtful. When he was approached, he brushed off the hurts as their fault for not comprehending what he actually communicated.

> *Acceptance, significance, and security are all passions of the soul and have strengths but, when overdone, are destructive to oneself and others.*

Over time, he found himself being marginalized by the group of leaders. People were unwilling to work with him and didn't want him in their group. He was just difficult to work with, and conflict seemed to follow him around. Eventually, he got a job out of state and moved. Interestingly enough, his new job allowed him to use his detailed research and knowledge to address the issues of social injustice around the world. I suspect that his work requires little teamwork and more research than is reported to a leadership team.

If the soul, wired for security, uses its strengths to build its self-worth, it will find itself wanting more control and having things their own way. Just like the other parts of the soul, strengths become overdone. The demanding spirit comes out. Things must be done their way. Why wouldn't anyone not want to do things the right way? Fear for not doing the right things can cause much anxiety.

The clearest biblical character wired for security from my perspective is Luke. He was a doctor who was meticulous in writing down the Gospel and the Acts of the Apostles. He was well researched and did it for the glory God.

The soul's anatomy has three parts. Each part of the soul is a reflection of the image of God. Acceptance, significance, and security are all passions of the soul and have strengths but, when overdone, are destructive to oneself and others. When we use our motivational drives to achieve self-worth, we can develop a demanding spirit. If we are successful in achieving self-worth through the three passions of the soul, we construct idols that demand to be fed. And they are never satisfied. They don't result in love for others because we are so focused on achieving our own self-worth. In John 15:12–13, the apostle taught us that love is always for the sake of others: "Love one another just as I have loved you. No one has greater love than this—that one lays down his life for his friends."

Acceptance

Significance

Security

Reflection Questions

1. What are the things that you do that give you a sense of self-worth?

2. Relate the story of the pastor who used his strengths to achieve self-worth to your story. As you reflect on your story, can you identify how you achieve self-worth apart from God's love?

3. Which passion of the soul can you most identify with? Passion for acceptance, significance, or security? Share why.

14

Soul Anatomy
and Love

So we have come to know and to believe the love that
God has for us. God is love, and whoever abides in
love abides in God, and God abides in him.

—1 John 4:16

The three passions of the soul as discovered by Porter (he called them the three ways we achieve self-worth) explains why we behave the way we do. The empirical evidence is in. Over two million people have been as-

> When God created man, he created him in his image. He created him as a relational creature who had the capacity for love. He was created to love and receive love.

sessed, and they agree that the three passions of the soul is the best explanation of their behavior. There is a very good reason why this is so. Porter's theory based on self-worth is closely related to the teaching of Scripture on love. Love and self-worth are cousins.

God is love. Earlier in the book, we systematically made the case that the foundational and primary attribute of God is love. All the other attributes of God extend from love. Even the holiness of God is an extension of his love. The law is subsumed by keeping the law of love. God is best described as supreme love. God is relational, and his love is perfect in the persons of the Trinity—Father, Son, and Holy Spirit. They are in perfect peace, harmony, agreement, and unity. He is worthy of our worship because he is love.

When God created man, he created him in his image. He created him as a relational creature who had the capacity for love. He was created to love and receive love. He was created to love God fully and completely. He was created to receive the love of the Trinity, who was perfect. This was the design of God for man. This was his garden identity prior to Fall. Human souls had their need for love completely met by their creator God.

> *Since the Fall, the human soul has been craving the love that was lost. God never stopped loving.*

Because God's love was received by Adam and Eve, they did not need to strive after his love. It was freely given. God was lavish in his love, demonstrated by his incredible provision in the garden. Every need they had was completely and satisfactorily met by God. 1 John 4:16 declares, "So we have come to know and to believe the love that God has for us. God is love, and whoever abides in love abides in God, and God abides in him." John was stating this truth for those who have been born again, but this was true in the beginning at creation in the garden. Adam and Eve had an abiding relationship in his love. The plan of salvation as described in Scripture is a plan to return to that which was at the beginning. The goal is to restore the garden identity of man—abiding in the love of God.

Since the Fall, the human soul has been craving the love that was lost. God never stopped loving. The Scriptures are the story of God pursuing man. He has an everlasting love (Jer 31:3). It was man who rejected the love of God. He chose another way and has been chasing it ever since. The soul was designed for love, the love of God. Nothing else will ever satisfy. The hole we have in our souls is a hole created by our sinful nature that seeks self-worth/love apart from God. Our thirsty and hungry souls are craving for the love found in the garden.

Christian Comaford wrote about this craving in *Forbes* magazine, "In every communication, in every conflict, we are subconsciously either reinforcing or begging for safety, belonging, mattering or a combination... It's neurological... it's primal... there is nothing you can do to override or change this subterranean subconscious programming as much as you may try."[30] As believers, we don't believe that our situation is hopeless and unchangeable. But we recognize the truth of our wiring for self-worth/love. The difference is that we believe that through the Gospel, we can know and live in the fullness of God's love and therefore do not need to be controlled by a demanding spirit that never finds satisfaction.

We have a keen sense that this love is available, and we search after it in every corner of the universe. We demand it from other people. The chief reason we have so much strife and agony in our relationships is that our relationships are based primarily on trying to extract the love we need from other people. Over and over again, we are disappointed that other people fail to love as we want, as we demand. You see, the craving for love is not just a desire; it is needed for survival.

I was working with a pastor who was traumatized by his parent's divorce when he was going through puberty. His memories of that time were vivid. The verbal arguments and physical altercations continued over years before the entire family. The parents were unable to love the children effectively during this time, leaving them feeling vulnerable and unsafe. They wondered if they were significant to their parents, who were consumed with other things not understood by them at the time. When the divorce finally took place, the typical struggle of who gets who and for how long ensued. The feelings of rejection and despair sent arrows of resentment and confusion deep into the souls of the children.

This man's wounds experienced as a child have shaped his world. Even though he now has a perspective on what happened and has forgiven his parents, his behavior is such that it is clear that he is still chasing after the

> *Our souls are shaped by how we strive after love. We choose different paths, but each of them lead to nowhere.*

love for his soul that is a deep hole. The pattern of thinking that demanded a different way to be loved than he experienced colors every decision and even every encounter with other people. Each person on his personal journey is an opportunity to extract the love he didn't receive in his childhood.

In an unconscious but very real way, he is asking the following questions: "Am I accepted by you? Am I significant to you? Am I safe?" If there is a hint that any of these questions are not in the affirmative, his demeanor changes. He becomes defensive, fearful, and tense. Shame and guilt lurk beneath the surface. You can see the change in his eyes and stature. He is quick to defend and attack, lest he allows himself to experience the pain he had as a child.

Unfortunately, this man has been unable to sustain himself in the role of pastor as he was trained and so desires. You can imagine the pain that has been created in those who have been cared for by someone who is not secure in his own soul. Having been fired numerous times, the spiral of pain has taken root. It is a bitter root that is destroying his soul. Self-worth and love is something that we were created for, and without it, we chase after it.

> *God's plan of restoration of the human soul is to return us to our garden identity where we were created for love and we experienced the fullness of God's love.*

Our souls are shaped by how we strive after love. We choose different paths, but each of them lead to nowhere. Some choose achievement and success, hoping that they will be seen as worthwhile. Others choose the path of nurturing others in hopes of securing other's love. Still others choose the path of doing things right and proper. We reason (consciously or unconsciously) that if we are careful and do things well, we will be safe. When we are successful, we feel loved. When we are not successful, we strive and demand it by doubling down and overdoing our strengths.

This pursuit of love that is needed and desired leads us to a very selfish life. Life is about me and what I need. Often I need it from you. When we read the definition of love in 1 Corinthians 13, we are overwhelmed by the lack of selfishness in love. It is selfless. The need for self-love, however, is demanding of others. But the love of God is extravagantly giving.

God's plan of restoration of the human soul is to return us to our garden identity, when we were created for love and we experienced the fullness of God's love. Romans 5:5b teaches us that "the love of God has been poured out within our hearts through the Holy Spirit who was given to us" (NIV). The love of God is available to those who have been reconciled to Him through Jesus Christ. Our hearts/souls can know the love of God, and we can live in the presence of God's love through the gift of the Holy Spirit that dwells within us.

Discipleship, if directed at the soul, the place that drives behavior, must focus on the passions of the soul. We can teach a biblical worldview and have adequate theology, and if we don't deal with the passions of the soul, we will be disappointed in our discipleship. If we focus on building Christian character and the fruit of the Spirit, and we don't deal with the passions of the soul, we will find ourselves making little progress. The soul is the seat of decision-making, and it is driven by the need for love. When we can articulate the passions for the soul and identify what is driving our mind, emotions, and behavior, we will have the opportunity to see the sanctification process move much more quickly.

In the diagram below, you will see the three-motivational drives or passions of the soul. This diagram adds additional truths that are useful in our understanding love. I am amazed at the fluency many Christians have about the words used for love in Scripture (agape, philia, eros), but I believe we still lack a paradigm for understanding love and its nature.

The Soul is shaped by three passions

The illustration is a picture of how we give and receive love. This is critical to understand. If this is true, it gives us a clear path to the discipleship of the soul.

A part of the soul pursues self-worth/love through caring and nurturing others. We have labeled this core passion as "acceptance." We want to be accepted, not judged. We want to be included and not isolated. We want to belong. Our soul wants to be embraced in community and doesn't want to see others excluded. Our soul wants to be accepted by others. That warms our soul, and we feel loved. We long for this warmth and embrace both physically and emotionally. Even sexually.

The part of the soul pursuing self-worth/love through accomplishment and getting things is labeled "significance." Our soul does not want to be invisible. We want recognition because we want to matter to others and be significant. When the soul does something that contributes movement and goal achievement, it feels valuable and important. The bigger the contribution, the more valuable and significant the soul feels.

Another way the soul seeks to love is through safety. The soul motivated for safety strives in doing analysis and doing things right, and in a fair and consistent manner. We have labeled this passion of the soul "security." The soul feels secure when we are doing the right things in the right way. We want to be safe and secure. We avoid risks and make sure that danger is avoided.

The three passions of the soul are acceptance (belonging), significance, and security. These are the means by which we know love and offer love to others. We are designed by God to give and receive love as we are created in his image and bear his image. These three passions of the soul are always at work. Either we will pursue these three passions by receiving love from God himself as we were designed, or we will pursue these three passions of the soul by seeking love from other things. The goal of discipleship is to build self-awareness of what is driving their soul and to point people to Jesus. Only Jesus Christ, the perfect lover of our souls, can meet the needs that we genuinely are seeking.

Let us demonstrate that these three passions of the soul truly are the way we experience and give love. If you love your wife, you will embrace her no matter what she does. You accept her as she is and don't need to change her. She doesn't need to become more acceptable. You nurture her and care for her like your own body (Ephesians 5). She belongs to you. She wears a ring on her finger to let others know she belongs to you. She experiences your care and acceptance as love. She is drawn to you because she is fully accepted by you. She can open up to you and reveal her deepest secrets because there is no shame. She belongs to you and nothing will change that.

She is the most significant person to you. If you love her, she will not feel invisible or unimportant. She will feel like the most important person in your life. When she enters the room, you perk up and take notice and are excited to see her. The football game you were watching pales in comparison to her presence. She is significant to you, and your world is ordered in such a way that she knows it. She experiences your focus and attention as love. She knows she is the most important person in your life.

If you love your wife, you will keep her safe and secure. Love protects. You make sure her needs are met. You defend her if she is threatened because love makes sure they are safe. Your wife feels love from you when you do these things for her. Your provision and watchful eye on her demonstrates that love. She feels safe and secure in your arms. She has a sense of freedom because with you, there is no fear. She is safe.

The women who are reading the above descriptions of what it means to be loved are saying, "I wish I had that!" As human souls who have sinful natures, we love imperfectly. We don't always express the three ways love is given and received well. But God is perfect in his love. His love never fails (1 Cor 13:8). He is the only source of love that we can rely on, no matter what. His love is amazing!

Our lives will be transformed when the three passions of our soul have their focus on the One who is able to love perfectly. Are we convinced that God has accepted us and freed us from guilt and shame? He doesn't despise me. He loves me. Galatians 2:20 states, "I have been crucified in Christ, the life I now live, I live by faith in the Son of God who loved me and gave himself up for me" (NIV). I don't like it when people treat me in a way that I am not accepted or don't let me into their group. But I am okay because the God of the universe has fully accepted me. I am a child of the King! I have a new identity. I have been grafted into the family of God. The old self is dead, and Christ lives in me. I don't like being left out and not being invited at times. But I don't demand an invitation because I am loved by God and have the acceptance of the Christ. This fills my soul. In fact, it fills my soul to overflowing and enables me to accept others who don't do anything to satisfy my need. My needs are filled to the brim. If I don't get a call to that church that I had hoped to pastor, I don't become despondent from rejection. My soul is still full. I am trusting God to direct my steps.

If we are fully convinced that God's love is what brings me significance, when I fail in a project, my soul is not destroyed. I don't have to blame others to feel better about myself or push harder and run over those who blocked my path to success. Others may have hindered me and challenged my leadership, but I continue to love them because my soul is full and overflowing. My identity is not diminished. Even if I am not recognized for my contribution, I can rejoice with those whose contribution was celebrated. I am basking in God's love, which is perfect, and his plan will not fail. I see my life in perspective to the plan of God and what he is doing in the world.

And this is the plan: At the right time he will bring everything together under the authority of Christ – everything in heaven and on earth. Furthermore, because we are united with Christ, we have received an

> *Our lives will be transformed when the three passions of our soul have their focus on the One who is able to love perfectly.*

inheritance from God, for he chose us in advance, and makes everything work out according to his plan. (Eph 1:9–11, NLT)

We are convinced and trust that God had made us secure. I feel safe. No matter what happens, I know God's love will carry me through. Nothing will separate me from God's love. Romans 8:35–37 addresses this question,

> Can anything ever separate us from Christ's love? Does it mean he no longer loves us if we have trouble or calamity, or are persecuted, or hungry, or destitute, or in danger, or threatened with death? (As the Scripture say, "For your sake we are killed every day; we are being slaughtered like sheep.") No, despite all these things, overwhelming victory is ours through Christ, who loved us." (NLT)

Not even stage-four cancer can shake my confidence in God's love. I ache for parents whose children are chasing drugs and living a lifestyle that leads to destruction, but I am trusting in the love of God to sustain me.

I am willing to risk everything for Christ because in obedience to God's call, I will not fear or shrink back. I am safe in the arms of Christ. I don't need a 401(k) plan that is overflowing or a paid-off mortgage before giving generously to my church or the mission project of our church because my security is not in those things. I feel free because I have cast off fear: "Perfect love expels all fear" (1 John 4:18).

Can you see the power of discipleship that focuses on the three passions of the soul? These three passions for love can only be met in Christ. He is inviting and waiting for us to enjoy his love and walk in it. His love is transforming.

Reflection Questions

1. How has your soul been shaped by the way you were loved/not loved in your childhood? Tell the story.

2. Love has three faces. We often only think of love as a feeling or affection for someone. When you reflect on the three faces of love, what is most important to you?

3. Think about the love of God. How have you experienced God's love (using the grid of the three faces of love)?

4. What problems are you facing (what are your fears and what causes you to worry), and how might that change if you fully believed that God loves you (three faces of love)?

15

The Soul in Church History

*Most of us were taught that God would love us if and
when we change. In fact, God loves you so that you can
change. What empowers change, what makes you desirous
of change is the experience of love. It is that inherent
experience of love that becomes the engine of change.*

—Richard Rohr[31]

When you look into historical references on the soul and how different periods of church history addressed discipleship, you will find commonalities. Let me give a sampling of how others in the past have viewed the soul in relationship to discipleship and sanctification. As we review just a few of these, you will notice that there are some differences, but there are also some similar convictions. Of course, we cannot be complete or be exhaustive in this short chapter about how the church has historically viewed discipleship. That would be a fun journey, but our purpose is simply to show that the ideas being presented in this book are not totally new or novel. They reflect the thoughts and practices of the church going back to our early church fathers.

Desert Fathers

The Desert Fathers were early Christian ascetics and monks who desired to live more closely with God and live in holiness. They were often extreme in their approach to eradicating the fleshly nature. Generally speaking, they lived in the Scetes desert of Egypt. The most known of the Desert Fathers was Anthony the Great, who is known as the founder of desert monasticism. The eastern monastic tradition at Mt. Athos and the western Rule of St. Benedict both were strongly influenced by the traditions that began in the desert. All of the monastic revivals of the Middle Ages looked to the desert for inspiration and guidance. Much of Eastern Christian spirituality, including the Hesychast movement, had its roots in the practices of the Desert Fathers. Even religious renewals, such as the German Evangelicals, the Pennsylvania Pietists, and the Methodist revivalists in England, are seen by modern scholars as being influenced by the Desert Fathers.

These Desert Fathers are credited for the development of a discipleship tool called the Enneagram. The Enneagram is used to help people related to one of nine personality descriptions. This is done by asking participants to examine six paragraphs of personality descriptions and choose the two that is most like them. By the way, this test known as the Riso-Hudson Test was formed very recently and has not historical ties at all. Once this is done, one can look to see a description of that personality and the adjoining sin that often accompanies that personality. There is also a description of that personality in nine levels of functioning (healthy to unhealthy or with Christ reigning in the life or Christ not reigning in the life).[32]

The use of this test has helped many identify the dominating sin in their life. It has also helped them to find the solution to the sin—Jesus Christ. Each identified sin has the potential to replace our identity in Christ. For instance, I am an achiever personality, and my accompanying dominant sin is deceit. In an effort to gain approval or to feel valuable, truths are stretched, etc., to influence others of my worth. The desire to be valuable can deteriorate into chasing after success. This information is helpful to me in identifying blind spots in my life. If we explore this a little further in prayer, we may even discover historical events in our past (hurts for example), which have shaped our personalities. The achiever personality is often a slave to this sin. Only Jesus can rescue them. Jesus is the only one who can declare us of value and acceptable by his work on the cross. That understanding changes not only my relationship with Christ, but also the motivation of my life.

Renee Roserio is a top expert on the use of the Enneagram. She claims the greatest value of the Enneagram is to understand the three motivations that produce personality and behavior. She labels these motivations worth, approval, and security. Notice the close connection between the terms she uses to describe the motivational underpinnings of the soul of man to the motivations of the soul that we have been proposing: acceptance, significance, and security.

The reason she says it is so important that we recognize the three motivations behind the formation of the Enneagram instrument is because real transformation comes only when we get back to the root cause of behavior. I find this fascinating because the Enneagram is best known for identifying sinful behavior rather than motivational drives. Her point is that identifying the behavior has little value if you don't get behind what is the motivation behind the sin.[33]

Augustine (354–430)

Augustine is probably the most quoted theologian in history other than John Calvin. Yet Calvin most often quoted Augustine as he was foundational to his thought. He is often depicted in classical art holding the church in one hand and the human heart in the other. He believed that you cannot know God if you don't have self-knowledge of your heart. His most famous quote is "Know thyself!" He was obviously a student of the soul.

His theory about sin and discipleship is based on what he called "disordered love." In this theory, he believed that the focus of discipleship should not be on behavior, bad deeds, or actions, but rather on the love of God. The keystone of this theory is that the soul must find satisfaction in God alone and nothing else.

The idea of disorder comes in when he suggests that there are three objects of our love: love for God, love for others, and love for ourselves. This is also the order that he believes God would have our souls aligned.

He taught that if our affections are stronger for anything other than God himself, our lives will be in turmoil, for we were created to love God. Closely related to this idea is the concept of idolatry. Idolatry is love out of order. It is when something is more important than God and essentially displacing Him from the throne of your life.

Although Augustine's thinking is not identical to the thoughts we are presenting, you can see that the love of God is front and central to his concept of discipleship. You will also recognize the replacement of satisfaction in God with satisfaction in other things and people. Also note that Augustine had little interest in trying to do behavior modification. He was convinced that this was a waste of time. The problem for him was that love was misplaced. I believe his teachings are compatible to soul discipleship as being presented in this book.[34]

Ignatius of Loyola (1491–1556)

Ignatius was a Spanish knight from a Basque noble family. After having a serious wound, he had a spiritual conversion and devoted himself to God, following in the order of Francis of Assisi. He is best known for forming the Society of Jesus or the Jesuits. His *Spiritual Exercises* is still used widely as a means of discipleship around the world.[35]

The foundational principles behind his exercises are what he called the three passions of the soul. He believed that the soul was controlled by three powers or affections. Interestingly, these three passions of the soul are acceptance, significance, and security. He believed that these three affections of the soul are what drive sinful behavior. In order to free yourself from these affections, you must identify them and then use the exercises that he put together, which include readings, meditations, fasting, silence, and other spiritual practices. Many of the exercises are based on stories in Scripture that relate to these affections of the soul.

Ignatius believes that the three passions of the soul cause what he called "inordinate affections." This is when we attach our souls to things that cannot satisfy. They are idols of the soul that must be detached. We do this through the exercises. The exercises are set up in four-week increments. Gradually, the affections are loosened as we grow in our love for God. The three passions of the soul are redirected to God and away from the things that were wrongly attached.[36]

Again, we can see the similarity of Ignatius's approach to discipleship. He has his focus on the soul, which is the motivational center of one's being. He goes after the why rather than the what. He identified the same motivations of the soul as we have discussed in soul discipleship. Much of his approach is focused on inside-the-cup discipleship rather than outside the cup.

We have looked at three short periods of church history and have found some common understanding of what is the source of sinful behavior. All three approaches focus on the inside or soul rather than behavior. What is common to all is the understanding that if we are captured by the love of God, our souls will be transformed and so will our outward lives.

Before leaving this quick historical review, I would also say that there are beliefs and practices of each of these historical approaches to discipleship that the author would not endorse (i.e., self-inflicted pain to kill the flesh). However, I believe that the common ideas presented show that there are some foundational truths which we would be foolish to ignore at our own peril.

Reflection Questions

1. Do you recognize the pattern of historical Christianity and how discipleship was addressed? What is its significance for us today?

2. Why do you think the twenty-first-century approach to Christianity is a departure from historical Christianity?

3. What are the issues that keep us from returning to a historical and biblical approach to discipleship that includes self-awareness of what is driving the soul and a focus on the reorientation of the soul to find love?

16

The Soul Has a Shell

*Why are you talking about having no bread? Do you still not see
or understand? Are your hearts hardened? Do you have eyes but
fail to see, and ears but fail to hear? And don't you remember?*

—Mark 8:17–18

If you have any experience at all in discipleship, you will discover quickly
that the soul has a shell. Around the soul, there is a hard and difficult protective barrier that makes it difficult to penetrate. That shell is resistant to
the truth, is unwilling to change, and is committed to self-protection. If you
are going to be a discipler of the soul, you are going to need to understand the
nature of the soul's shell and how to break through it.

I was a youth pastor in a rural town outside of New York City. We hosted
an open gym night every Friday for the youth of the community, as there was
very little to do in the area. One night, a girl came in dressed more like a guy,
accompanied by eight other friends dressed in black with black makeup. Her
exterior was as hard as her interior. She wore black jeans with a chain attached to her belt. Her black motorcycle boots and black shirt completed the
look. She looked tough, and she was tough. She could curse up a storm if you
looked at her the wrong way. She was both there and not there at the same
time. She was illusive when approached, but she kept returning. Something

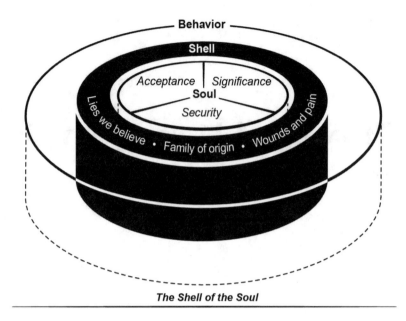

The Shell of the Soul

was attracting her to form a relationship and open up, but emotionally, she was distant. It was clear that she had a drug problem as she smelled like weed and was often stoned when coming to the open gym. Her persona gave me some clues that she was not comfortable being a woman. She kept everyone at a distance, yet there was something soft inside that was reaching out.

One day, I received a call from Laurie. She was in jail. With tears in her eyes and stumbling for words, she said she doesn't trust anyone anymore in this world except me. Me? I barely knew her. Somehow she saw me as someone safe, and she was desperate. So I got in the car and went to the local jail to see what I could do for this lost soul. This would be the beginning of a two-year journey filled with frustration, pain, and joy.

When I got to the jailhouse, I discovered that she had been arrested for attempted murder, along with a long list of other misdemeanors. I sat and listened for an extended period of time while she would begin to open up and then shut down completely while she thought about how much to share with me. Gradually and painfully, the story of her life vomited on the table. It was difficult to conceive the life she was describing to me.

Laurie was born into a family where her father abused her sexually from the earliest times of her memory. Her father would beat her and threaten her to keep her from telling anyone. Then when she was twelve years old, "the only loving person she had known", her mother, suffered and died from cancer in just six weeks. Left to be raised by her abusive father, she began to look for a way out. Looking for someone to love her, she met a guy and slept with him the first night. That resulted in a pregnancy at the age of thirteen. Her father was furious with her and beat her up. She decided to get an abortion, one of many she would endure.

Eventually, social services removed her from the abusive home. She was assigned to a foster home where she was abused again sexually. This time, she would not stand for it, and she left. When I met Laurie, she was living in the woods alone. She would occasionally crash at someone's house, but she had no address, had dropped out of school, and was dealing drugs to stay alive.

The reason she was arrested was because a guy she thought liked her (another abuser) was discovered to have another girl in his bed. She went crazy and began to destroy his car with a baseball bat. The car was totaled, but her rage continued as she went after him. That is when the police showed up and arrested her. She told me she would have killed him if they hadn't arrived at that moment.

When I appeared in court with her for the hearing, I learned that her mother was actually a clerk at that same courthouse before she died. The judge wanted to help her, knowing her story. I volunteered to be that person to work with her, so they released her into my custody. There is much more to the story, including her trying to kill herself on the way home from the courthouse by jumping out of my car at sixty miles an hour. One night, she obtained a gun and had it to her head with the police at the door. Eventually she let me in (I still can't believe the police let me go in), and she gave me the revolver and wept.

I can't begin to describe the thickness of the shell around the soul of this young girl. The pain, the hate, forgiveness, false beliefs, fear, and anger were all layered on top of each other to form a heart of stone. Even though Laurie received Christ as her savior and prayed the sinner's prayer with all sincerity, she was resistant as anyone I have known to the discipleship of her heart.

Scripture on the Shell

As a result of the Fall, the soul has been resistant to the call of God. We hide in shame behind fig leaves. We form a worldview contrary to Scripture and reality. We are easily deceived, and darkness is preferred over the light. The shell of the soul exists both for believers and unbelievers. Just because you have become a follower of Christ doesn't mean that our shell has been dismantled. But here is the good news. God is at work going after your soul! Those God "foreknew he also predestined to be conformed to the image of his Son" (Rom 8:29).

The Scripture refers to the shell as a "hard heart" or "callous heart." Jesus often spoke about the shell. One time when the disciples had forgotten to bring bread with them, Jesus turned to them and said, "Why are you talking about having no bread? Do you still not see or understand? Are your hearts hardened? Do you have eyes but fail to see, and ears but fail to hear? And don't you remember?" (Mark 8:17–18). This event takes place near the end of Christ's earthly ministry. The disciples have been followers for a long time. But for some reason, they struggled to have their souls changed by the Gospel of Jesus Christ.

Two times in the past, Jesus had performed miracles that demonstrated His power to provide everything they needed. Jesus said, "When I broke the five loaves for the five thousand, how many basketfuls of pieces did you pick up?" (Mark 8:19). I can just picture the disciples mumbling the words under their breath, "Twelve." Then Jesus questioned them again, "And when I broke the seven loaves for the four thousand, how many basketfuls of pieces did you pick up?" (Mark 8:20). "Seven." Understanding comes hard to a hard heart. The truth doesn't sink in. We are committed to thinking outside the Gospel. The care of Jesus is just not understood. He is able. He really is! Yet worry and anxiety is par for many believers. The shell is thick. But it can and must be broken. You can't disciple the soul without dealing with what is making the heart hard.

Jesus uses another illustration to describe the hardness of heart—the shell of the soul. When speaking to Job at the end of the story, God likens Job's heart to that of a Leviathan (Job 41). Job could hardly be considered a rebel against God, but his soul was likened to some kind of wild animal. Some scholars believe what is described in this passage is some kind of giant crocodile. Others believe it is a mythical creature, like that of a dragon (breathes fire out its nostrils). Either way, it is a graphic description of the soul's resistance to being shaped by God.

Read God's response to Job's hard heart and think about your heart as you digest the metaphor:

Can you catch Leviathan with a hook
or put a noose around its jaw?
Can you tie it with a rope through the nose
or pierce its jaw with a spike?
Will it beg you for mercy
or implore you for pity?
Will it agree to work for you,
to be your slave for life?

Can you make it a pet like a bird,
or give it to your little girls to play with?
Will merchants try to buy it
to sell it in their shops?
Will its hide be hurt by spears
or its head by a harpoon?
If you lay a hand on it,
you will certainly remember the battle that follows.
You won't try that again!
No, it is useless to try to capture it.
The hunter who attempts it will be knocked down.
And since no one dares to disturb it,
who then can stand up to me?
Who has given me anything that I need to pay back?
Everything under heaven is mine.
"I want to emphasize Leviathan's limbs
and its enormous strength and graceful form.
Who can strip off its hide,
and who can penetrate its double layer of armor?
Who could pry open its jaws?
For its teeth are terrible!
The scales on its back are like[e] rows of shields
tightly sealed together.
They are so close together
that no air can get between them.
Each scale sticks tight to the next.
They interlock and cannot be penetrated.
"When it sneezes, it flashes light!
Its eyes are like the red of dawn.
Lightning leaps from its mouth;
flames of fire flash out.
Smoke streams from its nostrils
like steam from a pot heated over burning rushes.
Its breath would kindle coals,
for flames shoot from its mouth.
"The tremendous strength in Leviathan's neck
strikes terror wherever it goes.
Its flesh is hard and firm
and cannot be penetrated.
Its heart is hard as rock,

hard as a millstone.
When it rises, the mighty are afraid,
gripped by terror.
No sword can stop it,
no spear, dart, or javelin.
Iron is nothing but straw to that creature,
and bronze is like rotten wood.
Arrows cannot make it flee.
Stones shot from a sling are like bits of grass.
Clubs are like a blade of grass,
and it laughs at the swish of javelins.
Its belly is covered with scales as sharp as glass.
It plows up the ground as it drags through the mud.
"Leviathan makes the water boil with its commotion.
It stirs the depths like a pot of ointment.
The water glistens in its wake,
making the sea look white.
Nothing on earth is its equal,
no other creature so fearless.
Of all the creatures, it is the proudest.
It is the king of beasts." (NLT)

This description of the shell is not a passive response to the truth of the Gospel. This is active fighting against the truth. There is resistance that is fearsome. Like God says in verse 24, "Its heart is hard as a rock, hard as a millstone." But as you know, God does get through to Job. The shell was broken, and he opened his heart to what God had for him. He repents in dust and ashes. The breaking of the shell always results in repentance.

When God sends Jeremiah the prophet to bring correction to Judah, he likens their heart to tablets of stone: "Judah's sin is engraved with an iron tool, inscribed with a flint point, on the tablets of their hearts..." (Jer 17:1). I can't help but think about another tablet of stone that Moses was engraving with an iron tool on Mount Moriah. There is a comparison going on here between the Ten Commandments that are engraved on Moses's tablets and the sin that is engraved on the hard stone of their souls. The Gospel of Jesus Christ is forming a heart of love that will carry out the fullness of the law. But the soul is engraved (committed to) with sin.

The prophet Zechariah spoke to God's people, "But they refused to pay attention, turning away stubbornly and stopping their ears so they could not hear. Indeed, they made their heart as hard as diamond, so that they could not obey the Torah and the other words the Lord who rules over all had sent by his Spirit through the former prophets" (Zech. 7:11–12, NET). There is no harder element on earth than a diamond. That is the metaphor used to describe the human soul— the shell of the soul.

Jesus quoted from Isaiah 6:9–10 when he saw the resistance to his teaching amongst the religious leaders of his day. He called their hearts "dull." He referred to their "eyes being shut." Paul quotes from the same prophetic text in Acts 28:27 as he concludes the story of the Gospel being spread to the world. Along with the condemnation of those who have calloused hearts, there is a promise. The promise is that "those who understand with their hearts and turn, I will heal them." This is news of hope. We should not be dismayed in discipling those who have thick shells and hardened hearts. Don't give up! Jeremiah was encouraged by God not to give up, for "nothing is too hard for God" (Jer 32:17).

Paul, in writing to the Ephesian church, calls the believers to not live like the Gentiles of the world. It is a call to discipleship and call to leave behind what they once were:

> So I say this, and insist in the Lord, that you no longer live as the Gentiles do, in the futility of their thinking. They are darkened in their understanding, being alienated from the life of God because of the ignorance that is in them due to the hardness of their hearts. Because they are callous, they have given themselves over to indecency for the practice of every kind of impurity with greediness. But you did not learn about Christ like this, if indeed you heard about him and were taught in him, just as the truth is in Jesus. You were taught with reference to your former way of life to lay aside the old man who is being corrupted in accordance with deceitful desires, to be renewed in the spirit of your mind, and to put on the new man who has been created in God's image—in righteousness and holiness that comes from truth. (Eph 4:7–24, NET)

He uses the image of being callous. I am actually writing this book in a log cabin that I built with my own hands. It was the biggest challenge I have ever taken on physically. By the time I finished the project, my hands were callous. The skin had become hardened. First they were red and sore. Then they developed into blisters that eventually burst. Over time, the skin developed hard patches of thick skin a nail would have a difficult time getting through. This is the condition of so many souls. They have developed resistance to feeling and being responsive to the touch of God. Laying aside the old way of thinking and putting on the new man requires breaking through the callousness of our souls.

Laurie was eventually released by the court after trial into our custody, and she was placed in Teen Challenge in Brooklyn, New York. She lasted two days and then ran away. However, that is not the end of the story. We received a letter from Laurie after seven years of not knowing anything. She was living in Kansas working as a union carpenter on the road crew building molds for concrete barriers. She was living with an elderly Christian woman and being discipled by her. She thanked us for being the loving hands of Christ in the darkest part of her life. She thanked us for not giving up on her. The shell of her soul had been broken, and she let the love of God in. Love changes everything. It is not only the goal of discipleship. It is the means as well.

The shell of the soul by definition is anything that hardens the soul and keeps a person from knowing and experiencing the fullness of God's love. Both believers and unbelievers have a shell on their soul. In order for our souls to be changed, the shell must be penetrated or broken. We make a big mistake when we plow ahead in our discipleship and don't address the shell.

The soul builds defense mechanisms to protect itself. Laurie experienced great pain from those who "loved" her. As a result, she wouldn't let anyone into her life emotionally because she didn't want to experience that again. She found other ways of getting love or what she perceived as love—what gave her self-worth. The pain and emotional damage that was done in her soul resulted in the thickening of the wall. She couldn't open herself to the love of God or even to the love of a youth pastor.

Peter Scazzero of the *Emotional Healthy* series of books calls this the shadow side of our souls. He describes it like this: "Your shadow is the accumulation of untamed emotions, less-than-pure motives and thoughts that, while largely unconscious, strongly influence and shape your behaviors. It is the damaged but mostly hidden version of who you are."[37] The key issue here is that it is largely unconscious. That is what makes the shell so difficult to deal with. But be sure, we all have one.

It would be impossible to describe every way the shell is hardened and gets thicker. The soul is creative in protecting itself. Let me describe the big ones that show up continually in people's lives. You will recognize some of these in the lives of others and some that have impacted your own life. My intent is not to thoroughly address the issues of every shell that has developed but to simply help us recognize that we can't ignore it in discipleship. I do recommend Peter Scazzero's series of books on this topic as a more thorough approach to dealing with the issues and bringing to light that which is often unconscious. Another resource that is helpful is Dr. Ron Walborn's series of DVD training entitled *Personal Spiritual Formation*. In this book, I am more focused on showing the critical nature of dealing with the passions of the soul and the critical role they play in discipleship. Therefore, I will simply describe categories of issues that impact the shell, which protects the soul from transformation by the Gospel.

Family of Origin

The first category is what we will call issues caused by family of origin. We all have our own unique family experiences. Our worldview is greatly shaped by how our family sees the world and how we perceive ourselves. Laurie's family of origin is likely very different from yours. But you are just as impacted by your family as she was by hers. When I began dating my wife, I discovered a wonderful loving family that I embraced as my own. However, I soon discovered that they saw the world differently than I did. They were very cautious and fearful about most everything. My wife grew up in that environment, so she just thought that was normal. What she discovered was that I wasn't normal! My family didn't live by fear at all. I was raised to believe that you can do anything if you put your mind to it and you should go for it. The way we see life and live life is so different because of our family-of-origin issues. Sometimes, it takes someone outside of the family system to see the dynamics of what is happening because we have been so immersed in the family that we are in effect blind. But that doesn't make the wounds that were inflicted less painful and life-altering. Discipleship will require the examination of family origins to discover what wounds were inflicted, the walls that were built, and the habits that were developed.

Wounds and Pain

The psalmist wrote, "For I am ready to fall, and my pain is ever before me" (Ps 38:17). This is the experience of all who walk the face of the earth. Fathers disappoint. Loved ones walk away in anger. Injustice abounds. No one escapes the scathing burn of sin. The deeper the pain, the more profound the impact on our souls. Apart from the freeing work of the Spirit, wounds and pains misshape the soul. We strive after love through the passions of the soul, but ultimately, we are disappointed. Only God's love does not disappoint.

We stuff our pain and try to overcome our wounds by avoiding and hiding. We defend our souls by not letting others in. We don't take risks because we have a powerful memory of past hurts. We don't get too close or let people see what we are really like. The last time I did that, I was rejected and left alone. Past wounds and pain are powerful elements of the shell that make it difficult to get to the soft soul that needs so badly to be shaped by the Gospel.

Lies We Believe

Lies have many different sources. Sometimes that come from within us as a form of self-protection or a way of coping with the lack of love that we may feel. If you have ever viewed the television show *American Idol,* you will understand the level of self-deception that exists in the world. Do they really think they can sing? Why doesn't someone tell them they stink? I have a feeling many people have told them the truth, or at least have sent signals to take a different path, but they refuse to believe the truth. This is true of not just singers, but preachers, leaders, fathers, and employees. We want to believe things about ourselves that are not true. The shell must be broken.

Lies also come from without. A father tells his son that he will amount to nothing. He hears that perhaps ten times when his dad has a fit of anger. A thirteen-year-old girl overhears some friends talking about how "ugly" she is. Those poisonous words form roots in the soul that are not easily pulled out. We want to be loved so badly. We make up things that are not true, and we dwell on words that threaten our sense of being loved. These produce shame and hiding that thicken the wall of our souls.

There is a special kind of lie that we believe that is demonic. The devil is the deceiver. His nature is to lie and deceive. Sometimes our deception has its root in the demonic. Saul wanted to attack David when an evil spirit would come upon him. Saul was deceived in believing that David was a threat to him. The truth was that David would never touch the Lord's anointed.

As we disciple people, we must explore these three areas and address each one of them with the Gospel. Every one of these inflicts a heavy emotional component that can only be broken by the love of God. If we don't expose that which is hidden or unconscious, they will not be revealed, confessed, forgiven, or released. Ultimately, the Gospel teaches us that the love of God is sufficient to break the chains and bondage of sin, the power of sin, and the consequences of sin.

One more thought on the shell of the soul that is critical to understand and that we should not bypass: it is possible to expose and reveal what the shell of the soul is made of and try to address it apart from the passions of the soul discussed in this book. There may appear to be relief from pain for the moment because it feels good to let out the pain or to place blame on someone who has hurt you. Or it soothes the pain when others understand what I have endured. But our goal is not to relieve pain. In fact, the pain is a tool that God can use to make them desperate to understand the fullness of God's love. Only God's love will satisfy the longing of the soul for love. The goal of the discipler is to help the disciple recognize their need for love as expressed in the three passions and must find their satisfaction only in God's love.

The breaking of the shell of the soul is a work of the Spirit. It is not a work of excellent counseling or a technic of spiritual healing. I am reminded of the story of the disciples who came back frustrated that they could not cast out the demons. Jesus responded with these words, "This kind can come out only by prayer" (Mark 9:29). Some manuscripts say "prayer and fasting." Just as casting out demons requires the finger of God, so does the breaking of the soul's shell that has been hardened after years and years of pain, wounds, lies, and habits. We will need to teach disciplers how to pray and hear the voice of the Holy Spirit. The Spirit of God will clean the house and put things in order. Praying and fasting is not a shortcut to discipleship. But it is the only way the soul can be set free to love.

Richard Rohr describes the liberation that must take place (breaking the shell):

> True liberation is letting go of our false self, letting go of our cultural biases, and letting go of our fear of loss and death. Freedom is letting go of wanting more and better things, and it is letting go of our need to control and manipulate God and others. It is even letting go of our need to know and our need to be right – which we only discover with maturity. We become free as we let go of our three primary energy centers; our need for power and control, our need for safety and security, and our need for affection and esteem.[38]

Richard calls the passions of the soul "our primary energy centers." The shell is attempting to achieve love without letting go. It is trying to make sense out of life apart from God and his perfect love. It will always fail. And that is why the Gospel is so powerful. It offers hope to those with no hope. We really only have one thing to offer those who have been beat up by our world and our own sinful nature—the powerful love of God as demonstrated in the person of Jesus Christ on the cross. But that is all any of us need.

Reflection Questions

1. How is the church impacted when we fail to understand the shell of the soul and it-remains unbroken in the disciple's life?

2. Think about your family of origin. Are you aware of family-sin patterns? How have they impacted you?

3. What wounds and pains have you experienced, and how have they impacted your soul?

4. Can you identify the lies in your life that have persisted to keep you from experiencing the fullness of the love of God? What are they?

PART III

Discipling the Soul

We become free as we let go of our three primary energy centers; our need for power and control, our need for safety and security, and our need for affection and esteem.

—Richard Rohr

17

Broken to Love

*How precious is your loyal love, O God! The
human race finds shelter under your wings.*

—Psalm 36:7

Disciples who are captured by the love of God are transformed. We embrace our new identity as a child of God. We desire to love like him and live out his priorities. Our wounds are healed and fear dissipates. Love is powerful!

Just look at the lives of the disciples. These men were full of self-love and self-focus. One of the most bizarre conversations in Scripture is when James and John come with their mother to Jesus and ask if they can have the seats on the right and left of Jesus when he is ruling the kingdom (Matt. 22:22). Now that is self-focused! I can see why John left that story out of his Gospel account! It was a low moment. Here, you have an argument that develops between all the disciples about who is the greatest. To some extent, the disciples were following Jesus to get ahead for themselves rather than for the love of God and his kingdom. That radically changed forever.

At the end of the book of John, after the resurrection, Jesus meets up with the disciples in Galilee. He prophetically pronounces that Peter is going to die if he chooses to "feed my sheep." The passage is quite graphic, and

Peter has no doubt as to what it means. "Very truly I tell you, when you were younger you dressed yourself and went where you wanted but when you are old you will stretch out your hands, and someone else will dress you and lead you where you do not want to go" (John 21:18). That was a nice way of saying that Peter will be crucified just like Jesus was crucified. History tells us that Peter was crucified, but upside down because he didn't think he was worthy to be killed like Christ. Now that is transformation—from wanting to rule and be better than everyone to willingly dying so others can hear the Gospel of Christ.

You only make that kind of change when your love changes. Before the crucifixion, Peter denied Christ three times, just as Christ said he would. He even was afraid to testify that he knew Jesus before a harmless servant girl. That was a low point of shame. Peter had declared his loyalty over everyone else just hours before. It turned out that he loved himself more than Jesus. But that all changed.

Perhaps everything changed for Peter when Jesus asked him three times to feed his sheep (once for each time he failed to respond before). Maybe that was a healing moment for him. Jesus still wanted him on the team. He still belonged. He was significant to Jesus. Jesus trusted him and even prophesied about how his life would end (that doesn't sound "safe or secure" but it was for Peter). Peter was entrusting his life to Jesus and his care. All his need for self-love was dying. The love of Christ was all he needed. He was free to serve God.

> **The early church expected their disciples to be willing to die for their faith.**

When I speak with pastors about their disciples and what their discipleship process is producing, they universally say that they are not producing disciples like Peter, or Paul, or Thomas, or others who were sold out to Christ and willing to do whatever God called them to do. In other words, we have few, if any, disciples who love God in a similar way as these saints. The early church expected their disciples to be willing to die for their faith. They had to love God more than themselves (find the love they needed in God alone). Death was a good possibility. The stakes were higher.

This thing called love is a big deal. If we had just a little idea about how great the love of God is for us, we would be changed too. If our soul was filled by the love that God has for us, we would be set free to change the world. The statistics of how many people claim Christ as their Lord and Savior and what percentage of that number have ever told someone about their faith is embarrassing. Evangelism Explosion used to report less than 10 percent have ever shared the Gospel! Perfect love drives out fear. I guess we are not close to perfect in our love. Love is lacking.

Paul Tripp wrote a book called *Awe*.[39] The book looks at the many times the word *awe* and other synonyms that demonstrate the incredible surprise and response of the people who experienced the life of Christ in the book of Mark. The people were in awe of Jesus's power over nature. They were in awe of his teaching that was so different and authoritative. They were in awe of his healing power and compassion. Everywhere Jesus was walking, there were people with their jaws dropping to the floor.

Paul concludes that we don't have a sin problem in the church. What we have is an "awe" problem. We are no longer in awe of who Jesus is and what he has accomplished for us. We are ho-hum about God! The new iPhone release gets more jaws to drop to the floor. Paul argues that if we had more awe for God, we would lose our interest in sin. Our love for God would increase.

The greatest of all the attributes of God is his matchless love. We should be in awe of God's love. When Peter first got a clue as to the nature of Jesus when they were fishing out in the Sea of Galilee, he fell on his face and said, "Go away from me, Lord; I am a sinful man!" (Luke 5:8). He became aware of his sin in the presence of righteousness. Then Jesus invited him to be with him as a disciple. He invited him to belong. He accepted him, sin and all. So his journey began as he discovered more and more about the love of God.

In the middle of the Sea of Galilee, in the midst of a terrible storm that made even the most skillful and experienced fishermen believe they were about to sink, the disciples were awed by the power of the Son of God (Matt. 14). He walked on water, and he stilled the waves. They learned the love of God and its protection over their lives. Yes. He not only loves, but he has the power to execute his care and protection over those he loves. He can be trusted. He is great.

Remember when the Pharisees brought Jesus a woman caught in the act of adultery and paraded her before everyone? How did Jesus respond to this woman caught in guilt and shame? She was guilty for sure. She deserved to be stoned for her sin. Yet Jesus said, "Let any one of you who is without sin be the first to throw a stone at her" (John 8:7). Then he forgave her and told her to sin no more. The love of Jesus considered even this sinner, caught in the midst of sin that deserved death, as someone worthy of his compassion and forgiveness. We are significant in his eyes. Yes, he knows all our sins. Even the secret ones that you commit don't deter the love of God. Yet he calls us to himself. We can't impress him or earn his love. It is given generously and freely.

Are you in awe of God's love? Or has his love become commonplace and been diminished? Discipleship elevates the love of God in the disciples' life and helps them to grow in awe. Your growth in Christ will be proportional to your experience in God's love. Those who have been loved much love much.

> *Definition of love: Love lays down one's life for others.*

We have been discussing the love that God has for us. This is the essence of the Gospel—God so loved the world that he gave his only Son. The sacrifice of Christ on the cross is evidence of this spectacular love. No greater love is there than one lay down his life for his friends. This truth is the very definition of love: love lays down one's life for others. Love is not selfish. With this in mind, let us consider what Jesus taught about love and the qualification for being a disciple.

With massive crowds surrounding Jesus, he recognizes that not everyone who is following are true disciples. He begins to teach about what a true disciple looks like. He lays down some parameters or requirements for being a disciple. You will soon see that Jesus's requirements are much higher than most churches. It doesn't require "just saying a simple prayer." It is more than being sorry for sins. It has more to do with the heart/soul. He doesn't beat around the bush but is rather direct. So direct is his approach that many go away.

Jesus whittles down the crowd with this sharp truth: "If anyone comes to me and does not hate father and mother, wife and children, brothers and sisters—yes, even their own life—such a person cannot be my disciple" (Luke 14:26). Wow! I have never heard that kind of invitation at a crusade! It probably wouldn't draw many converts. It didn't here either.

Obviously, Jesus was not teaching hate. He is the Son of God and full of love. He is using a literary device to emphasize that a disciple will love Christ more than they love anyone, including themselves. He isn't telling people to stop loving others. That would be inconsistent with everything in God's Word. The end result of discipleship will be image bearers who reflect the character of God in the world, especially the love of God.

When we love anyone or anything more than Christ, we will compromise our obedience to him. In Luke 9, Jesus called out some wannabee disciples who had this issue. Jesus knew what was in the soul, even though the outward words appeared to be reasonable. A man indicated to Jesus that he would follow him wherever he would go. Jesus responded to his soul with this statement, "Foxes have dens and birds have nests, but the Son of Man has no place to lay his head" (Luke 9:58, NIV). Jesus saw that his soul loved the comfort of his home more than Jesus and that he couldn't be a disciple until he loved him more than his comforts.

To another man, Jesus asked to follow him. The man's response was, "Lord, first let me go and bury my father." Jesus's response again sounds harsh and inappropriate, but he is looking into the soul. His response is right on point. Jesus says, "Let the dead bury their own dead, but you go and proclaim the kingdom of God" (Luke 9:60, NIV). Please recognize that Jesus was not against funerals. He went to many of them. However, he usually raised them from the dead! My point is that

> **The first step in discipleship is to love God more than you love anything or anyone.**

Jesus was not being difficult or antisocial. The social situation for someone to leave and follow Christ might very well have meant being disinherited. It appears that is the situation here. This man wanted to follow Christ, but he didn't want to risk his inheritance.

In each of these situations, the soul's orientation was greater toward other things than toward Christ. The first step in discipleship is to love God more than anything or anyone. You must place your mission under the mission of God. Jesus said this often and in different ways. He said, "No one can serve two masters. Either you will hate the one and love the others or you will be devoted to the one and despise the other" (Matt. 6:24, NIV).

Jesus told the parable of the hidden treasure and the pearl with the same point. "The kingdom of heaven is like treasure hidden in a field. When a man found it, he hid it again, and then in his joy went and sold all he had and bought that field. Again, the kingdom of heaven is like a merchant looking for fine pearls. When he found one of great value, he went away and sold everything he had and bought it" (Matt. 13:44–46). God is of such worth that nothing compares. Nothing is worth keeping compared to the awe-inspiring love of Christ. If you are a disciple and you are not all in, you will not mature in Christ. You may grow in knowledge, but you will not mature in Christ. This is the first step in discipleship. If you are discipling someone whose love is divided, call them to the awe-inspiring love of God. Paint a picture of the full extent of his love. Help them understand that all their desires are met in the love of God and nowhere else. Like Christ, call them to be all in. You are calling them to life.

To love the Lord with all your heart, mind, strength, and soul is the call of God on our lives. It was the call of God on Abraham when he was raising up a nation to love him and show the world the way of love and worship of the one and true God. When God promised Sarah and Abram that they would have the joy of having a child (they had been childless), that promise was repeated over and over again as they aged past childbearing age. When the child was finally conceived and born, the child held a special place in their lives. If you know couples who could not conceive and the heart-wrenching pain that they endure, you might get a glimpse of what was going on in Sarah's and Abraham's soul. Finally! A beautiful son! That son held a special place in his daddy's heart. I've watched some couples that have finally been able to conceive, and that child is well protected and almost worshipped.

What was in Abraham's heart? Did he love this son more than God? God put him to the test. He asked him to go and take his beloved son and sacrifice him on the mountain. I can't think of a more difficult test for anyone to endure. God was asking Abraham to choose between his love for his son and his love for his God. He passed the test. He was obedient. He reasoned in his heart that God is such a great and loving God that he would somehow raise this child back to life! That is how much love that Abraham had for God.

God could entrust Abraham with great wealth and never question the orientation of his heart. He would possess many things—in fact, he was made a very wealthy man—but he would never be possessed by them. He loved God with all his heart. John Wesley once said, "Give me a hundred men who love God with all of their hearts and fear nothing but sin, and I will move the world."

A closely related and second step of discipleship is to deny yourself and take up your cross. Jesus said, "And whoever does not bear his cross and come after Me cannot be My disciple" (Luke 14:27). Also he spoke these words: "If anyone desires to come after Me, let him deny himself, and take up his cross daily, and follow Me" (Luke 9:23). The concept of denying oneself has often been misunderstood and misapplied.

> **To deny oneself does not mean to not care about your life or to not love yourself.**

It does not mean that we are to endure great burdens. The cross is not a burden to be carried. Jesus is not talking about carrying burdens or facing trials. We may face trial and carry burdens as a result of being a disciple, but that is not the idea here.

To deny oneself also does not mean to not care about your life or to not love yourself. It is popular to teach people that because they have a sinful nature, they should not love themselves. These same teachers instruct people that the greatest issue for disciples is that they love themselves too much. I think that is a misapplication and distortion of the Scripture. To not love the person God loves does not make sense to me. To demean the value of God's creation, which is made in his image, is foreign to Scripture. Even after the fall, God declares that he loves us with an everlasting love (Jer. 31:3).

I believe to deny oneself and pick up your cross is to die to your personal mission and submit yourself under the mission of Christ. Remember, you can't live with two masters. One must die. The mission every soul is on is to find life and meaning apart from Christ. We are created by God for the need for love—acceptance, significance, and security. Self-worth is not a sin. It is more about how we try to meet those needs that causes us such pain and hopelessness.

Apart from Christ, we strive in life to achieve these three things. They dictate all our decisions. This is our mission apart from Christ. It is about meeting our own need for love. Needing these things is not wrong. That is how we were created. But we were designed for only God to meet those needs. Any mission to meet those needs apart from Christ will fail and lead to disappointment. Jesus said, "Whoever wants to save their life will lose it, but whoever loses their life for me will save it" (Luke 9:24, NIV). What we are looking for is only found in Christ!

Don't misunderstand what I am saying. I am not advocating a pursuit of self-love and using others for one's needs. Paul was correct when he described the last days: "But mark this: There will be terrible times in the last days. People will be lovers of themselves, lovers of money, boastful, proud, abusive, disobedient to their parents, ungrateful, unholy, without love, unforgiving, slanderous, without self-control, brutal, not lovers of the good, treacherous, rash, conceited, lovers

> *The result of dying to self is being free to live for the mission of Christ and the glory of God.*

of pleasure rather than lovers of God having a form of godliness but denying its power. Have nothing to do with such people" (2 Tim 3:1–5, NIV). What Paul describes in this passage is a person who is trying to meet their need for acceptance, significance, and security apart from Christ. This description is a detailed and accurate picture of the person who may think they are a disciple, but in truth, they have never experienced the love of God. Their need for love is desperate and empty. I still maintain, however, that to teach people that it is wrong to have the need inside us to be loved or to have self-esteem is not helpful and misleading. It is pursuing this need in the wrong way that leads to death. That way must die.

The result of dying to self is being free to live for the mission of Christ and the glory of God. Here is how Tozer summarizes this truth: "In every Christian's heart there is a cross and a throne, and the Christian is on the throne till he puts himself on the cross; if he refuses the cross, he remains on the throne. Perhaps this is at the bottom of the backsliding and worldliness among Gospel believers today. We want to be saved, but we insist that Christ do all the dying. No cross for us, no dethronement, no dying. We remain king within the little kingdom of Man's soul and wear our tinsel crown with all the pride of a Caesar; but we doom ourselves to shadows and weakness and spiritual sterility."[40]

Jesus not only requires that we die to ourselves but that we forsake everything we have. Jesus said, "So likewise, whoever of you does not forsake all that he has cannot be My disciple" (Luke 14:33). He wasn't saying that we must give away everything and live in poverty, but he was speaking about our attachment to things and their use for our own mission.

A rich man approached Jesus and said, "What must I do to inherit eternal life?" (Mark 10:17, NLT). Jesus answered, "You know the commandments: Do not murder. Do not commit adultery. Do not steal. Do not testify falsely. Do not cheat. Honor your father and mother." "Teacher," the man replied, "I've obeyed all these commandments since I was a child" (Mark 10:18, NLT). Jesus was moved by this seeker, for the Scripture says he had genuine love for this man. He knew what was in his soul even before he made the following statement: "'–You lack only one thing,' He told him. 'Go and sell all you have and give money to the poor, and you will have treasure in heaven. Then come, follow me.' At this, the man's face fell, and he went sadly away because he had many possessions" (Mark 10:19–22, NLT).

The rich man could not forsake what he had. Too much of his acceptance, significance, and security, was tied up in his barns. He couldn't trust the Savior to love him and provide for him. This man looked into the eyes of the loving Savior, but he chose not to be a disciple. This is the case with so many people. This is why it is so hard for a rich man to enter the kingdom of God. They believe that the life they have will achieve their goals, but it always ends in emptiness. This was the testimony of the richest man in the world, Solomon. All of it is worthless.

Reflection Questions

1. Are you in awe of God's love? Why or why not?

2. How do you know that you are loving God with all your heart, soul, mind, and strength? What is the evidence that we, our passion of our soul, are no longer to be loved because we have the love of the Father?

3. If to die to oneself means that we have as our focus the mission of Christ, how are you seeing that in your own life, and how are you challenging your disciples to die to oneself?

4. How does your ministry of discipleship resemble or not resemble the discipleship of Christ?

18

Orphan Spirit

I will not leave you as orphans; I will come to you.

—John 14:18

For the next few moments, I would like to invite you into the world of being an orphan. You are on your own. You don't have anyone who considers you "theirs." You have nothing to depend on. You may even be without a place to sleep. You have no home. Who is going to fight for you? Just you. You must strive and struggle through life and do the best you can to make a name for yourself. Your future is uncertain and filled with fear and anxiety. All of these—homelessness, despair, broken trust, separation, and alienation—are why these words of Jesus are central to the Gospel: "I will not leave you as orphans; I will come to you."

Recently, I was in Asia doing some training with oversees workers on understanding the orphan spirit. My own understanding was deepened through this experience as I met a couple who had adopted three Chinese children and added them as beloved children to their three natural-born children. The last of these orphans adopted had only been with them for three weeks!

It was fascinating to watch this newly adopted orphan come to grip with no longer being an orphan, now having a loving family that was smothering him with love. He was about ten years old. Most of his life had been lived out in an orphanage in China. He was institutionalized because no one wanted him. He had issues. He wasn't acceptable to anyone, not even his parents. I know little about the facility or professionals who were raising this child or the hundreds of other rejected children. I am sure they cared for him the best they could.

Who knows what was going on in the mind of this child? He was once a numbered inmate in an institution, but now he was in a family. As I observed, it was clear that the love of the mother and father was overwhelming to him. Their patience when he was screaming or carrying on by crying was palpable. And it wasn't the parents alone. The three children were just as engaged in loving their new brother.

We were together for nine days, so I observed this budding new relationship for approximately a little more than a fourth of his new life in the family. In that short time, you could see the progress of trust. In the beginning, no one could touch him or hug him. It was uncomfortable and threatening. Tantrums and a demanding spirit were commonplace. Apparently, that was how he got what he needed when in the institution. You could see fear in his eyes. *What is happening to me? Is this for real?*

At the end of the nine days, we were swimming in a pool with this entire family and saw major shifts in behavior. Yes, there were still tantrums like that of a three-year-old, but now he was responding to the love of his mother. He excepted her embraces and listened to her words of encouragement and correction. The tantrums were shorter. His eyes were brighter. He was frolicking in the pool with his brothers and sisters.

To make this experience more difficult for this young child, all this took place in the context of a five-star resort. Imagine living in an institution with gray walls and little stimulation and suddenly being thrust into an environment with an acre swimming pool, waterslide, and fountains! His room was plush with the lavish and luxurious appointments appropriate for wealthy Westerners to travel in a plane for twenty-four hours just to experience for a week. The food was offered at a never-ending buffet. Whatever you want, you can have it! It was overwhelming for this orphan who had little, who had to fight for attention, and who lived in fear.

But he was no longer an orphan. He was a beloved son! He was beginning to experience the full love of parents who love him unconditionally. He is now a child of privilege. His old way of behaving, however, is largely unchanged. There are new understandings developing. Something has changed. But many things remain the same. As he experiences the love of the father, his understanding and outlook in life will change. Behavior will also change as the love of the father will change his heart. This newly adopted orphan is still struggling to discover if he belongs, if he is secure and significant.

I hope this true story will help you gain a full-color picture of how most souls experience life apart from Christ. The soul has experienced life as an orphan since the fall in the garden. Apart from the love of the Father, life is uncertain. It is lonely. It requires an aggressive posture to be noticed and be important to someone, anyone.

Some people are more successful than others in achieving the acceptance, significance, and security that they so desire and need. Perhaps they are better at dancing or throwing a football. They experience success and the praise of others. They feel good about themselves. They start a business that catches on, and it becomes a franchise. The reward of their work gives them power. Money can buy acceptance, significance, and security. Or can it? You are witty and fun to be around. You learn that when you joke around and throw a party, people like being around you. The more successful they are at meeting these needs through their gifts and talents, the greater their self-worth.

Others are not so fortunate. You see, the world is pretty competitive for getting on top. In the process, the less talented, the less attractive, and awkward people are pushed down. Climbing the ladder means climbing on others. I can remember feeling horrible when I was cut from the baseball team. I felt worthless, rejected, and stepped on. It made me work harder next time because I didn't like that feeling of rejection. The shell of my soul was thickening. I hate feeling like an orphan, so "I will never fail again." My shell is thickened by my repetitive success. I don't need God to meet my soul needs. I am getting my needs met in other ways. Failure and success thicken the wall. It is how I learn to make it work in an acceptable way. The orphan spirit is a driver of so much of our behavior.

When our shell thickens, our ability to risk and be real decreases. We lose *our* ~~are~~ ability to be vulnerable and open our heart. We develop a persona as part of this protection of our soul because our soul is an orphan. Remember Laurie? Her persona as a "tough guy" was simply her shell being made manifest to the world. She has learned to be independent. Orphans depend on themselves for their mission—you can't trust anyone else.

When the orphan spirit is unchecked, it can grow into a habit and structure of thinking. The shell can become more like a fortress with a moat and crocodiles. Only a profound and experiential encounter with the presence of God can break through the gates. But the love of God can displace it. He did that for Laurie.

Jack Frost calls this orphan spirit the *shortcut spirit* because we can achieve our needs and mission (our mission is to achieve self-worth) apart from Christ and his mission. Jack defines the orphan spirit as "a person who feels that he or she does not have a home or a safe and secure place in a father's heart where he or she feels loved, accepted, protected, affirmed, nurtured, and disciplined."[41]

The Scriptures use sonship as metaphor to help us understand our relationship with God more than any other metaphor. My favorite sonship passage is Romans 8:14–17:

> For those who are led by the Spirit of God are the children of God. The Spirit you received does not make you slaves, so that you live in fear again; rather, the Spirit you received brought about your adoption to sonship. And by him we cry, "Abba", "Father." The Spirit himself testifies with our spirit that we are God's children. Now if we are children, then we are heirs – heirs of God and co-heirs with Christ, if indeed we share in his sufferings in order that we may also share in his glory.

Are you a slave, or are you a son? Paul declares that those who are justified by Christ are given his Spirit and are made sons, sons of God. We will discuss much more about the role of the Spirit in soul discipleship because the Spirit is the means by which God accomplishes his purposes in our lives. An entire chapter is dedicated to exploring the Spirit's role and how this impacts our approach to discipling the soul. But here, the emphasis is simply on the fact that something new and dynamic has taken place at our redemption. God placed is Holy Spirit within us! His life lives in us. That changes everything. Apart from this life-giving Spirit, we would be dead in our sins and powerless to live a life of love.

What a contrast Paul draws for us between being a son and being a slave. We were once all slaves. Slaves live in fear, uncertainty, and they must prove themselves every day and have no permanent home. They are only valued for what they can do. They have no inheritance. That is what we once were. We were a slave to our own need for self-worth. The heavy chains of striving after acceptance, significance, and security were wearisome. Life was driven by fear because nothing was sure or dependable. There was no true resting, for our work was never enough.

> **Orphans have a habit of meeting their own needs and live independently.**

Then God made us sons by his Spirit. He made us children of God. He adopted us just like that family in Asia adopted that little boy. Now we cry, "Daddy." Every moment of every day, the Spirit of God is testifying to our spirit/soul that we are his children. Can you hear the voice of the Spirit? Or are you still living like a slave?

Sons have privileges. They are unconditionally loved, and therefore, they will always belong, be important, and be safe. The Father is good and great. Nothing can separate us from the Father's love. The embrace of the Father is very different from the chains of a slave. They produce different kinds of behavior. Unconditional love is always a better motivator than fear, guilt, and shame.

Jesus himself taught us to approach God as sons and daughters. "Our Father"—now that sets the tone for our relationship. As a community of the children of God, we have access to the One who sits in heaven on the throne and is ruling the world. We are not slaves or orphans. We are sons and daughters. We can freely ask and receive from our Father's hand. We belong to the Father (our Father who art in heaven, forgive us our sins). We find our significance in his mission (thy kingdom come, and thy will be done). We find our security in his care (give us this day our daily bread, keep us from temptation). Prayer is the means by which we converse with our Father and receive his embrace of love. Orphans have a habit of meeting their own needs and live independently. They must learn new patterns of living, including abiding in the love of God through prayer and other competitive practices. We need to continually hear the voice of God.

Reflection Questions

1.   How do orphans live differently from sons?

2.   Can you identify with the orphan spirit? If so, in what way? If not, why not?

3.   How successful have you been in achieving self-worth apart from God? How has that hindered or helped you in your pursuit of God as your loving Father?

4.   The "shortcut spirit" (orphan spirit) is named as such because it is a shortcut to finding the solution to our love need apart from the pursuit of Christ. Can you identify how the shortcut spirit has revealed itself in your life?

19

Overcoming Temptation

*Then Jesus was led by the Spirit into the
wilderness to be tempted by the devil.*

—Matthew 4:1

The Christian life is full of temptation. You can't drive down the road without seeing an image of a provocative woman on a billboard luring you away from your wife. Everywhere there are images declaring that meaning is found in having something you don't have right now. Whether in the workplace or school hallway, there are people inviting you to experience the pleasures of the flesh that will ultimately destroy you. But that is not all of it. There is a spiritual world with actual spirits who are enemies of God and his people, who have it as their mission to destroy your life. Paul warns us, "For we are not fighting against flesh-and-blood enemies, but against evil rulers and authorities of the unseen world, against mighty powers in this dark world, and against evil spirits in the heavenly places" (Eph. 6:12, NLT).

Let us not look behind every door for a demon to blame our sin, but let us also not be ignorant about the spiritual reality of the demon world. Let us not ascribe to him greater power than the power of Christ and the Holy Spirit, but don't make the error of underestimating the role of the demonic world in our lives just because it is unseen. Paul was speaking about the danger of demons and their attacks to Christians, not to the unsaved.

Peter likens the devil to a prowling lion that is roaring and looking to devour you (1 Pet. 5:8). His warning is to "stay alert!" because we live in a dangerous world. We have a great enemy, and his ways are deceptive and cunning. He is full of deceit and fraud (Acts 13:10). He perverts the truth and the ways of the Lord. The devil is a liar and in fact is called the father of lies (John 8:44). Who knows what lies the devil whispered into Judas's ear to cause him to betray the Son of God with such boldness? The devil and his demons are laying snares and traps along the path of life to catch you. John warns us that the devil will actually cause us to suffer and test us.

But actually, our greatest enemy is our own flesh! The fall corrupted the hearts of men so that our bend is toward evil rather than good. Paul stated it like this, "For the desires of the flesh are against the Spirit, and the desires of the Spirit are against the flesh, for these are opposed to each other, to keep you from doing the things you want to do" (Gal. 5:17, ESV). The prob-

> *His plan is to take the bite out of the dog!*

lem is not just outside influences that cause us to sin, but actually, the biggest issue is what is inside our souls. Our soul is attracted to that which the world and the devil is offering because it has been corrupted.

There was a dog that had a terrible biting problem. He had bit several people in the neighborhood, but he was loved by his master. He did everything he could to break the dog of this habit, but everything he attempted resulted in failure. Finally, he decided to keep the dog muzzled. The dog had to wear a strap contraption restricting his ability to open his mouth, keeping him from biting anyone or anything. This was effective in keeping the dog from biting. However, it didn't take the bite out of the dog. Understand? There are many things we can do to muzzle our sin, but that is not God's purpose in discipleship and sanctification. His plan is to take the bite out of the dog!

The believer has the common experience of wanting to do the right thing and please God, but there is something within him that is battling against it. Paul recounted his own experience: "For I know that nothing good dwells in me, that is, in my flesh. For I have the desire to do what is right, but not the ability to carry it out" (Rom. 7:18, ESV). The flesh is the problem.

But there is good news. Jesus Christ! The Gospel of Jesus Christ sets us free from the law of sin and death. It is only because of Jesus that James can declare, "Resist the devil and he will flee from you" (James 4:1, NIV). Here is the promise in God's word that you have hope: "No temptation has overtaken you that is not common to man. God is faithful, and he will not let you be tempted beyond your ability, but with the temptation he will also provide the way of escape, that you may be able to endure it" (1 Cor. 10:13).

If that is true, why do so many Christians struggle with temptation and sin? If God has provided a way of escape, why do people continue to live according to the flesh? Why are so many people living in bondage? If God has fully provided for us the way out, and God is faithful, then perhaps there is something wrong with the way we are teaching people about how to resist the devil.   Most of us have been around the church for a long time and have heard the predominant teaching about how to overcome sinful temptation. It goes something like this: stay away from places where temptation abounds. Usually, a story about Joseph fleeing when Potiphar's wife grabbed onto him is told as an example to how we should avoid sin. There is nothing wrong with avoiding temptation if that is possible. Another technique that is taught is to memorize Scripture. "Hide the word of God in your heart so that you will not sin against God" (Ps. 119:11, NIV).

Certainly, memorizing and meditating on Scripture is useful in the battle against temptation. After all, most temptations are lies of Satan, so we need to know and focus on the truth. Prayer is another remedy for temptation that is offered to the struggling sinner. Asking God to protect against temptation is in the Lord's Prayer, "Lead us not into temptation, but deliver us from evil" (Matt. 6:13, ESV). If one fails and sins, the disciple is instructed to repent and turn away from their sin with sincerity and remorse, and they will be forgiven (John 1:9). Sometimes the teaching is accompanied by the explanation of "sincere." "Sincere" means that you are not just sorry about the consequence of sin but that you hate your sin and will not return to it. Lastly, the disciple is asked to choose an accountability partner to hold them accountable to living righteously. This partner is given permission to ask about the recurrence of that sin and other sins in the disciple's life. If you are from a charismatic background, you may also address the spirits (territorial, familiar, etc.) that are hindering a deliverance from the recurring sin.

I am not criticizing these means of overcoming temptation, but I believe we need to go deeper. Perhaps there is something going on in the soul that has yet to be addressed. If we don't deal with the root issue in the soul, why would we expect freedom? If we keep dealing with the outside of the cup, we will reap little in the way of righteousness. Let's not dispense with clear biblical teaching on overcoming sin, but let us consider how these instructions in Scripture can be used in a much more profound way.

In order to grasp temptation at a deeper level, I would like for us to examine the temptations of Christ from the perspective of what we have learned about the soul and its need for love. Remember, the soul was created for love and to love. We were created to be image bearers of the holy, loving God. The Gospel is God's love providing a way for us to be redeemed and living this image-bearing life. Life lived in the flesh seeks out love from everyone and everything apart from God's free gift and provision.

> *If we don't deal with the root issue in the soul, why would we expect freedom?*

Immediately after Jesus was baptized by John, he was led by the Spirit of God into the wilderness. Jesus was full of the Spirit of God. There was nothing in him of the flesh even though he had flesh like all men. He did not have a sinful and fleshly nature. He had just heard the words of God the Father pronounced over him at his baptism, "You are my beloved Son; with you I am well pleased" (Mark 1:11, ESV). Jesus knew the full and perfect love of the Father. It was in the context of this perfect love of the Father that he was thrust into the wilderness and experienced the temptation of Satan himself.

I find it fascinating that the Spirit of God chose to record for us in Scripture three accounts of temptation that appear to correspond to the three passions of the soul. The three passions of the soul are the three ways that we give and receive love: acceptance, significance, and security. You might miss this truth if you read the Scripture without the lens of the three passions of the soul.

In the first temptation, Satan comes to Jesus and seizes on the fact that Jesus is extremely hungry. He has been fasting and walking in the desert for forty days and nights. *Hungry* is an understatement if there ever was one! I'm currently on a five-hundred-calorie-a-day diet and think that I am hungry even as I am writing this book. But Jesus was literally starving. Most doctors would counsel Jesus never to do such a thing because it wasn't healthy. I had a friend who was a heavyweight wrestling champion in high school in New Jersey who fasted for forty days. He was identifying with Jesus in his fast. When I saw him, I didn't recognize him. He was skin and bones. He was weak but stronger than ever, spiritually.

In this state of hunger, Satan tempts Jesus by saying, "If you are the Son of God, command this stone to become bread" (Luke 4:3, ESV). Be certain that Jesus could have done as he was tempted as he truly was the Son of God. He could have chosen to do for himself what he wanted and needed by way of a miracle. But he rejected the tempter and said, "It is written, 'Man shall not live by bread alone'" (Luke 4:4, ESV). Jesus was quoting from Deuteronomy 8:3. Matthew quotes the rest of the verse: "But by every word that proceeds from the mouth of God."

The context is important to understanding Jesus's response. Jesus is in the desert/wilderness, just like the Israelites, when they came out of Egypt. There is a parallel here. It was the Spirit of God that led the Israelites out of Egypt and into the wilderness (pillar of fire and the cloud). God did this to find out what was in their hearts (ch. 8, v. 2). They failed this test as they did not trust God to provide for them what they needed when they needed it. God was faithful and provided manna, meat, and water for his children; but Israel didn't trust God.

Jesus is tempted in the exact same way, but he knows the love of God and that he is a beloved son. God will care for him. He doesn't have to provide for himself but will wait on the word of God. He will only do what God tells him. He knows he belongs to God (cared for as a son). His response to Satan demonstrated that in his heart, he was not tempted even in this extreme hunger because he trusted in the care of his Father. Obedience was possible because he trusted in the love of the Father for his care.

The second temptation takes place when Satan takes Jesus to the top of a high mountain. We don't know where this is, but from this mountain, they can see the kingdoms of the world in all of their "splendor." Satan claims that all the kingdoms on earth belong to him. He is the one reigning on earth. He then makes Jesus an incredible offer. He offers him all the kingdoms of the world if he would simply bow down and worship him. Now think about this. What is Satan appealing to in this temptation? If you were being offered to be the king and ruler of all the world, what within you would respond to such an offer?

A student who is trying to become the valedictorian of his class faces the hardest finals of his college career. This exam is the only thing that may come between him and this recognition. Suddenly, he is offered the test by a classmate who stole the exam, which would allow him to cheat and prepare. He chose to cheat. Why? He cheated because he so desperately wanted to be recognized. He wanted to be significant in the world's eyes.

There is nothing in the heart of Jesus that this temptation would have appealed. Jesus responded, "You shall worship the Lord your God, and him only shall you serve" (Luke 4:7, ESV). His significance was in worshiping and serving his Father who loved him so much. This was his purpose. This is what gave him joy. Jesus said, "'My food,' said Jesus, 'is to do the will of him who sent me and to finish his work'" (John 4:32, ESV). The passion of his soul was to find pleasure in doing the work of the Father. The worship or honor of men held no attraction.

I experienced a similar temptation as a church planter early in my ministry. We had just started a new church. We had all kinds of needs, especially money. About one hundred people had begun to attend this new fledgling church, but few gave anything, and most were not followers of Christ yet. There was a group of believers that came all together and told me how much they loved the church and the preaching (that appealed to my ego for sure) and that they wanted to make the church their home. They let me know that all ten families were great tithers and that they were excited to join the church. Then came the *if*. They would come if... then they presented their demands.

The culture of the church that we had planted was designed to reach people who had never darkened the door of a church before. We didn't do things like other churches. And God was blessing it. Eighty percent of our worshippers would come from the harvest for the first five years of the planting of the church. What this group of people was asking me was to change the church to make it more comfortable for them. For me, I would have had to give up what I believed God had called me to do. My soul was passionate to serve my God and obey, but my flesh was passionate about being successful! Success was an attraction to my soul... I'm not going to lie. I also like to eat! I didn't immediately say no to them. I went home to pray about it. God wouldn't let me go. This time, temptation was defeated because I wanted the praise of God more than the praise of men. The next year would be difficult and slow. Each week, my associate pastor and I would begin the week by asking whether or not we should get a part-time job driving a bus.

I wish I could say that my need for significance never kept me from living for the praise of the Father alone. There were failures. But even in those failures, the love of the Father was never taken from me. To love the Father is to know the love of the Father.

The last temptation recorded for us is when Satan takes Jesus to Jerusalem and to the very pinnacle of the Temple and tells Jesus to throw himself off. Satan quotes the Scriptures, "He will command his angels concerning you, to guard you," and "On their hands they will bear you up, lest you strike your foot against a stone" (Luke 4:10–11). Here you have Satan taking Jesus to a place of great danger and asking him to throw himself down into danger. Jesus responds to this temptation by quoting from Deuteronomy 6:16, "You shall not put the Lord your God to the test, as you did in Massah."

Again, context is important in understanding why Jesus quotes this Scripture. Massah is another name for Meribah. It was where the people of Israel complained to Moses that they had no water. Exodus 17:7 sheds some light on this, "And he called the name of the place Massah (and Meribah), because of the quarreling of the people of Israel, and because they tested the Lord by saying, 'Is the Lord among us or not?'"

The temptation of Satan was for Jesus to doubt the protection of the Father over his life. Is the Father really going to protect you? Is he going to be there when you need him? Test him! Throw yourself from the building and see if it is true? There was nothing in Jesus's flesh that questioned the love of the Father and his protection over his life. He didn't need to throw himself off the temple to find out if the Father is faithful. He was able not to sin even though he was tempted in every way as we are (Heb. 4:15).

In college, I signed up for a mountain climbing course to meet the requirement for physical education. I thought we were going to go hiking in the mountains and perhaps some weekend backpacking trips. When I received the syllabus, I learned that we had to purchase some "webbing" and a "carabiner." I didn't think much of it and went to the nearest sporting store and purchased the items, not understanding why these items would be needed in a hiking course.

The first night of the course (we met at 9:00 p.m.), I learned that this was not a mountain climbing course; this was a rock climbing course. We learned one knot that night and were driven to a hundred-foot cliff and was told to "throw yourself off!" Well, not exactly throw yourself off, but repel off the cliff. It seemed the same to me. I was not fond of heights. I had a childhood experience when I was just ten years old when my father made me go on the roof of a three-story building and held a step ladder for him, which was on a steeply angled roof. I thought, for sure I would kill my father. I had nightmares about falling off that roof for years. I hated going even near the edge of anything high, let alone dangling from a rope, in the dark. By the way, it was raining too.

To make matters worse, the instructor called out my name to go first. Perhaps she saw the confidence in my eyes. Actually, by the time I was in college, I had mastered the camouflage of fear by putting on a persona of strength. Inside, I was scared to death. Then to make matters even more frightening, my instructor handed my belay safety rope to the smallest, skinniest, most frail person in the entire college. She weighed about eighty pounds and was anorexic. Seriously. She was making a point. Her point would be made at my expense.

As I inched over the cliff (*centimetered over* would have been more accurate), I said a prayer and leaned backward as instructed. I couldn't see anything below me as it was pitch-dark with no moon in sight. The instructor assured me that the rope was long enough, and the little girl could hold my weight if necessary if I were to fall. I didn't believe her. I continued to inch my way down. When I got down about thirty feet, I heard the instruction to just let go. I said, "What!" The command came back with great force, "Just let go." I can't even let go when dancing, let alone dangling from a cliff in the dark when it is raining, by a rope held by a weak little girl who had no experience in belaying anyone. Plus… what if the rope breaks? How many times has this rope been used? It looked pretty thin. Well, I let go… for a second. I was okay. Then I let go for ten seconds, and she did hold me, even though I am sure I felt the rope slip a few feet this time.

After about fifteen minutes on the rope, I was able to trust the rope and the person belaying me and actually began to enjoy myself. I was bouncing off the cliff in ten-to-twenty-foot intervals. Before the course was completed, I would enjoy climbing three-hundred-foot cliffs that were rated 5.9 out of 6 (6 being perfectly vertical with no handholds or leaning backward). I learned to trust the rope and the person belaying me… even in the midst of fear. The fear never completely went away, but I learned to work through it.

We have a passion to be safe and secure. The only person we really trust is ourselves. We make decisions and organize our life to make sure we are safe. We hardly need to trust God because we have provided everything we need for ourselves. We are passionate about being safe. We are tempted every day not to trust God. Living by faith requires that we really believe that God loves me. Love is experienced through his loving and gracious watchful eye over our lives. But we will never know his love without obedience and trust. He will never let go of the rope.

Life can actually become less anxious and worrisome when we know the love of God and the security of his arms. We learn that obedience requires risking, believing that God will be there when we can't protect ourselves.

The three passions of the soul—acceptance, significance, and security — are all addressed in the three temptations that Christ faced on earth. Jesus was tempted in every way as we are (Heb. 4:15). Did he experience every temptation that we were tempted? Maybe. Maybe not. But surely, he experienced temptation like ours in every way. He experienced grief, shame, betrayal, hate, injustice, rejection, physical pain, and loneness. However, every temptation is ultimately a temptation to fail to love God and others. Remember, sin is a failure to love. All temptation is really about trying to get you to not love God or others. If you love God with all your heart, soul, mind, and strength, you will trust God to care for you, protect you; and that the most meaningful and purposeful use of your life is to live in obedience to him.

If you want to take the bite out of the dog, not just stop the dog from biting, you will need to disciple the soul. The way we deal with temptation will need to go deeper than we have before. We will need to get at the root and motivation of why we are so susceptible to temptation. We will need to clean the inside of the cup, not just the outside. We will need to have our minds renewed about the love of God.

So how does memorizing Scripture, fleeing temptation, prayer, accountability partners etc., fit with the passions of the soul? Each of these prac- tices has biblical roots, but if we use them mechanically, we

> *When we walk in our sonship and know the full extent of his love, we no longer have an attraction for the substitute that Satan offers.*

will only achieve stopping the dog from biting—for a while. If you want to take the bite out of the dog, these practices must address the soul and its pas- sions. We must apply the word of God to what is going on in the soul—our motivations. We must pray with awareness of the depth and deception of our soul—the false beliefs that hold us hostage. We need fellowship and account- ability that preaches the Gospel to be used constantly so we can strengthen our muscles of faith and be corrected and challenged when we are pretending. And fleeing from sin is not very effective unless we are running into the arms of a loving God. Develop your love for God. The kindness of God is much more effective in drawing us to repentance than the law of God (Rom 2:4; Tit 3:4).

Ultimately, the problem in overcoming temptation is dealt with through abiding in the love of Christ. When we walk in our sonship and know the full extent of his love, we no longer have an attraction for the substitute that Satan offers, that our flesh used to crave, or what the world teaches us. We know anything short of God's love is shaky at best and ultimately will fail us.

Reflection Questions

1. Why do so many people struggle with the same temptations for much of their Christian life?

2. What temptation Christ underwent that you most clearly connect with? Which temptation is the least attractive to you? Why?

3. How do the three passions of the soul relate to you in overcoming temptation?

4. How can you help others overcome their temptations? What practices do you need to include in your discipleship to help others successfully conquer Satan?

20

Reshaping the Soul

*When the disciples saw him walking on the water they were
terrified and said, "It's a ghost!" and cried out with fear.*

—Matthew 14:26

God is intent on transforming the soul. Like a blacksmith at the anvil,
the misformed iron is heated until it is pliable and moldable. Then the
iron is pounded and beat and shaped in such a way that in the end, it is un-
recognizable. But it must go through this process because it is not useful of
the purpose for which it was intended. The process is dangerous. The fire is
converted into a blistering furnace by forcing air into the embers so that it
can soften the hardest of metals. The sparks fly as a heavy mallet falls with
great force upon the softened substance. To harden the new form, the iron is
placed in a cold-water trough. The abrupt shift from heat and cold and back
to heat again is necessary to harden the steel being formed. Is that the story
of your life? It is mine.

Not to be overly dramatic, most of us can tell stories that resemble the
above description. The Scripture is full of these kinds of descriptions of purifying the souls of God's people. The most common image is that of the process of purifying gold through fire (Zech. 14:9, Ps. 66:10, Tim. 2:20–22). The
impurities of our life must be removed, and the process is not always pleasant.
We will all go through the refiner's fire during our life. It is in the refiner's fire

that we have the opportunity to join the Spirit of God in what is he accomplishing in our own lives and in the lives of others.

Walter Brueggemann proposed a way of understanding the Psalms of the Bible.[42] In his writings, he suggests that the Psalms are his most favorite and meaningful passages of the Bible because they are the real cries of the heart before God. Nothing is left out. They are raw and honest. When we read them, we can identify with the feelings the psalmist has penned.

Brueggemann suggests that the key to understanding and interpreting the Psalms lies in recognizing the three movements of the soul: orientation–disorientation–reorientation. The concept of orientation is that we all have a preconceived way the world is structured and works. Our soul is "oriented" around certain propositions. For example, we may believe that God will never leave me or forsake me. Our concept of that truth may be that I will never experience a life-threatening sickness or find myself without a way to support myself. Our orientation is the way we interpret life and see ourselves in relationship to our world and God. The most important constructs of orientation have to do with how our soul perceives itself—how it receives and gives love.

The idea of disorientation is when our orientation in life is threatened and no longer makes any sense. For example, if my orientation is that I will never experience a life-threatening illness, and I suddenly discover a lump in my chest, I may abandon my orientation. The doctor tells me I have stage four cancer, and they may not be able to treat it successfully. My life may now be in disorientation. My old orientation is no longer valid. It doesn't make sense of reality. Disorientation is often confusing and painful. Our view of the world that gave us meaning is no longer tenable. We look for solutions and cry out to God for help and understanding. For some, disorientation can

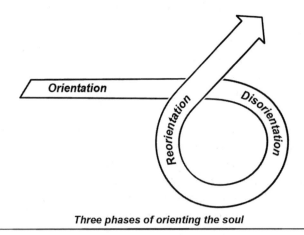

Three phases of orienting the soul

result in doubt and even running away from God. We can see this in the Psalms. The Psalms don't hold back during this time of disorientation. Accusations are thrown at God. Demands are made of God's justice. We need relief from our pain.

Over time we work through the disorientation that has been brought into our lives, and we experience a new orientation of life. This new orientation is called reorientation. We have a new way of interpreting our world and making sense of it. With the reorientation, we now have a way of dealing with our situation and return to a state of peace.

The cycle or orientation–disorientation–reorientation repeats itself over and over again as we go through life, as God shapes our soul. Discipleship of the soul is most available during the disorientation and reorientation phase. It is when the soul is most malleable and soft. It is looking for answers. And only Christ can make sense and bring about a reorientation of the soul that will satisfy. As disciplers, we should be keenly aware of these opportunities for the Spirit of God to do his soul work.

It is in these times of disorientation that false identities are revealed (if my wife leaves me, I am not loved, I am not a lovable person, I have little worth, I have no significance, etc.). The fact that our identity was never truly in Christ is suddenly uncovered and that we really never understood what it meant to be a beloved son or daughter of the King. The truth is that most of us say things we believe that we really don't believe. The blanket that has covered the truth of what we really believe and live out is only exposed when our false identity and belief is taken away. Then we feel naked and afraid.

> **It is in times of disorientation that false identities are revealed.**

Brian was in love with Victoria. They dated all the way through high school, and both were sure they would marry someday. They were both Christians and honored God in their relationship. They each pursued their career through different colleges hundreds of miles apart. In their second year of college, something changed for Victoria. She began to become aware that Brian was controlling and often put her down. He would compare his college with hers, making her feel inferior. She didn't like the feeling of being made to feel stupid all the time in conversation. At the same time, there was another guy treating her very differently. He was respectful and attentive. One day she broke off the relationship on the phone. After four years of relationship and plans to wed, the relationship was done. Brian was in turmoil. He came close to throwing himself off a cliff. His life was oriented around this one girl.

Now he couldn't make sense of life. Why live? Actually, the love of Victoria determined his worth. His acceptance was not oriented around Christ but around this relationship. Trying to hold onto this relationship, he became controlling. His value and significance was related to Victoria as well. This event started a journey or disorientation that led ultimately to his soul becoming reoriented around Christ and his love. It was a two-year journey of pain and questioning, but he discovered his sonship in a new way that he couldn't have known before.

The cycle of orientation–disorientation–reorientation has three narratives in Scripture. These three stories happen to attach themselves to the three needs of the soul: acceptance, significance, and security. This will become more obvious to the reader as they reveal themselves more fully. The three narratives are the (1) story of Job, (2) story of Solomon (Ecclesiastes), and (3) story of Joseph. These are fully human stories that we can all relate to and are helpful to navigating the disorientation of our souls. Only reorienting our souls around the love of Christ will ultimately satisfy.

Story of Job

The book of Job is probably the oldest book in the Bible and addresses the ageless problem of suffering. The story is about a man who is blameless and upright. In other words, the author is letting us know that everything that happens to Job has nothing to do with Job's sin. Great care is taken in setting up this very confusing situation of a good man having bad things happen to him. He was also a great man, respected in every way. He was the "greatest man among all the people of the East" (Job 1:3). It appears that he has God's favor over his life. Not only is he a great man, but he is a blessed man. He has seven sons and seven daughters and many people who work for him to take care of his vast herds of livestock. He was a deeply spiritual man as well. He prayed for his children and offered sacrifices for them, just in case they somehow sinned against God. He practiced spiritual disciplines like fasting over a period of time. The author goes to a great extent to let us know that this man should not expect anything bad to happen.

As you know, that is not what happens in the story. Everything that could go wrong goes wrong. And it all happens in one single day. Enemies came and put his servants to the sword. Before this report of calamity was finished, another report came that fire from heaven came down and burned up all the sheep and servants in the field. The way this is worded attributes the cause of the fire to God himself. Before this report was finished, another person came and told Job that three raiding parties came and took all the camels and killed all those tending them. By this time, you could imagine what was going on in Job's soul. If I were in his position, I would only be thinking about my children's safety. Apparently, they were feasting at the elder brother's house, so they were all spared. But then the word came that a mighty wind came on the eldest brother's house, and it collapsed, and everyone is dead. Wow! Perhaps you have had a bad day, but it couldn't be possibly worse than what Job experienced in one day.

Job's response was amazing. He simply got up, tore his clothes (grieving), and fell down in worship to God. You know the famous passage by heart that is often read at a funeral of a loved one: "Naked I came from my mother's womb, and naked I will depart. The LORD gave and the LORD has taken away; may the name of the LORD be praised" (Job 1:21). Even in his grieving, he did not sin against God or accuse God of wrongdoing. None of this brought about disorientation of his soul. His orientation was that God is sovereign and in control and that he alone was God. He would continue to worship God despite all that had happened.

Then his "friends" came along to "help" him. Most of the book is written about these friends' failure to grasp that God could have possibly allowed all these things to happen to a man unless he somehow failed God. Job was bombarded with a worldview that brought trouble to his soul rather than assist him in understanding the Father's love. Ironically, it was his friends who brought about the disorientation of his soul, not the actions of God himself.

The ending of the book brings about a reorientation of Job's soul. He can do nothing but marvel and submit to God when he comes to conclusion that he can't question God. He realizes that he is not God's judge, for he is just a mere creation of God. When his soul is reoriented, his life is restored even beyond what he had lost.

Job's friends had an orientation of their soul that could not fathom how a righteous and holy God could possibly allow a man to suffer and go through what Job went through—unless there was some hidden sin that needed to be revealed. Here was their orientation: God keeps people safe if they are righteous. He will not allow bad things to happen to good people. When we believe these kind of friends (or demons), we can easily get disoriented. Our soul is torn to pieces. We can't reconcile life.

Reorientation to truth and reality is that bad things do happen to good people. They even happen to upright and blameless people. The truth is that bad things are not necessarily related to our behavior. The reorientation that we must all work through in regards to suffering is that God is a good God and truly is sovereign. We can't understand the ways of God. And we can't tell God how to run his world. We know that in the judgment, God will make everything right. His judgment will address everything that was out of place. Our response to all the circumstances of life is to trust that God's love is the place of safety and security. It is dangerous to not trust in God and his plan for our lives. Romans 8 teaches us that nothing can separate us from the love of God.

As a pastor who is there for every tragic event in the lives of his flock, I can tell you that the process of orientation, disorientation, and reorientation is not an easy process to navigate. But I can also testify that it is in the pain of life that we learn to trust God for our safety rather than money, other people, position, and anything else that we substitute for the loving protection of our souls. We learn that life is not safe, but God can be trusted.

I love the testimony of Paul, who has no fear of man. He recounts all the pain and abuse that the world has thrown at him, including being shipwrecked, whipped, stoned, and left for dead, persecuted, and hated; and yet, he rests in the arms of Christ. He is convinced that in the end, Christ is the only one who will rescue him. Not even death itself can bring about fear. He has settled this issue and therefore was a fearless ambassador for the Kingdom of God. That is what I want for my soul. That is what I want for the souls of those in my flock. To come to place, I have to give up on trying controlling all of life. I am not God. I simply must obey the one who is God and trust his love.

Solomon (Ecclesiastes)

Solomon was both the richest man on the earth and the wisest man on the face of the earth. Rulers would travel from around the world to listen to the wisdom of this king of Israel. You could argue that Solomon was the most successful of all the kings who ruled in Israel. Under his rule, the kingdom was the strongest. His building projects were wonders of the world, whether it be the gardens he designed and built, or the temple that came to fruition after the death of David. The description of his wealth was unmatched in history (1 Kings 10:11–29).

His knowledge was knowledge of wisdom, unsurpassed. Listen to the account of the queen of Sheba when she visited Solomon:

> The report I heard in my own country about your achievements and your wisdom is true. But I did not believe these things until I came and saw with my own eyes. Indeed, not even half was told; in wisdom and wealth you have far exceeded the report I heard. How happy your people must be! How happy your officials, who continually stand before you and hear your wisdom! (1 Kings 10:6–8)

He was a true Renaissance man way before the Renaissance! He was also a driven man. He was tireless in his pursuits. He did everything with vigor, searching for meaning in life. Perhaps he is best known for the extent of his harem, which numbered one thousand, including queens from various nations of the world. Yes, some of them were marriage alliances for the protection of Israel (in violation of God's command), but Solomon thought that if he had enough beautiful women for himself, he would finally be satisfied.

At the conclusion of his glamorous and successful life, he writes the book of Ecclesiastes. If I were to title this book, it might be something like "Don't bother searching for meaning in anything because the pursuit is impossible." Or perhaps this title would fit: "Give up, and don't waste your time." Essentially, he is trying to help everyone who comes after him from wasting their life pursuing things that will never satisfy. After all, Solomon tried everything and in excess. If something had a promise of providing some pleasure, he would go after it. We would be wise to listen to what he has to say.

What was the orientation of Solomon's soul? He believed that he could find meaning through accomplishment and recognition. If meaning could be accomplished through accomplishment, Solomon would have been the person to achieve it. But in the end, he failed. He wasted his efforts and time. He concludes, "'Meaningless! Meaningless!' says the Teacher. 'Utterly meaningless! Everything is meaningless.'" (Eccl. 1:2). Not exactly a recommendation to follow his example!

The list of reasons why everything is meaningless is the content of this book. It serves as a warning to anyone with the orientation of seeking meaning in success and accomplishment. If you think you will find meaning in pastoring a bigger church, you're wrong. If you think you will find meaning in writing a book and having it published, you're wrong. You think if you work hard at your job, sacrificing for your boss and making bigger and better deals, you're wrong. If you think that if saving your money and traveling the world will fill that hole in your heart, you are wasting your time. Isn't Solomon encouraging?

Solomon systematically destroys each human pursuit that is meant to bring about meaning and purpose that satisfies. Your orientation may be on his list. Let's look at some of them. Are you pursuing knowledge and wisdom? How important is education to you? Well, Solomon came to believe that much wisdom brings greater sorrow and more knowledge, more grief. That was his experience. They disappointed him. Or how about seeking pleasure? Solomon sought pleasure everywhere it was promised and found it wanting. He thought if he could do great projects and have people serving him, he would find meaning. Nope.

If you think that working hard will bring satisfaction, Solomon shoots that balloon down too: "So I hated life, because the work that is done under the sun was grievous to me. All of it is meaningless, a chasing after the wind" (Eccles. 2:17). He learned that all hard toil brought was a loss of rest. The pursuit of accomplishment bringing about meaning was an empty promise. Don't bother. In the end, everyone will forget you and what you accomplished.

> *The emptiness and meaninglessness of all our accomplishments are disorienting to the soul.*

Riches too will disappoint. Finding meaning in wealth is empty. Here is his summary on this topic: "Whoever loves money never has enough; whoever loves wealth in never satisfied with their income. This too is meaningless" (Eccles. 5:10). He also found that the more you have, the more you lose sleep in fear of losing what you have. Of wealth, he is an expert, and he is very cynical about wealth's ability to bring about joy and meaning. He believes that God does not grant them the ability to enjoy what they have, but ironically, it is the stranger that has joy in your wealth instead of you (Eccles. 6:2).

You might come to the conclusion that life is a waste of time because the fate of everyone is death, and we are no more. But Solomon gives us some hope. In all the warning signs that he posts in this book about how meaningless everything is, he posts other signs that teach us that meaning is found only in relationship with God. It is God who gives the gift of allowing us to enjoy what we have. We can enjoy the toil as a gift from God as well, even though the accomplishment cannot provide it. What God is doing will last forever, so join him in what he is doing. No one can understand the ways of God or what he is doing, but we can trust him in this life that we can do and find joy in it. He concludes his book with these words, "Now all has been heard: here is the conclusion of the matter: Fear God and keep his commandments, for this is the duty of all mankind. For God will bring every deed into judgment, including every hidden thing, whether it is good or evil" (Eccles. 12:13–14).

The emptiness and meaninglessness of all our accomplishments are disorienting to our soul. We believe that in these accomplishments, we will find satisfaction, but we are always left wanting. We can have the world at our feet, and that will not bring about the significance we are looking to attain. For those of us with an orientation to success and accomplishment, we need to stop this useless pursuit. The more we believe these things will provide meaning, the more ruthless the pursuit becomes. Whether it is taking shortcuts by breaking the law, or running over people, or driving those who work for us to attain success, the promise is a vapor that appears only for a moment and is gone.

Solomon reoriented his life at the end. He learned that all of life must be about relationship with almighty God. In the end, only that which is eternal will last and have meaning. Charles Spurgeon commented, "Nothing teaches us about the preciousness of the Creator as much as when we learn the emptiness of everything else" (*Morning and Evening*, based on the English Standard Version). Solomon did not have the New Testament revelation that we possess. The mission of Christ has its fulfillment in the life to come. We are aliens in this life, and we are just passing through. Our home is in heaven with Christ. Our significance is found in the love of Christ. It is out of that love that we join Christ in his mission.

One more note of clarification needs to be made. We don't find our meaning and purpose in the mission but in Christ's love. If we seek significance in the mission itself, we will fail to find what we are looking for. This too is meaningless and empty. We serve Christ and his mission because we are fully significant and loved by him not to attain significance. Let's not confuse ourselves. I personally have this confusion in my soul as a pastor often. I can find myself feeling valueless when my ministry is failing or not as successful as someone else's. This is a sign that I have found my significance in something other than the love of God, which cannot be earned or deserved. The Gospel is the good news that we are loved (accepted, significant, and secured) because God chose to love us despite our unworthiness. We love him because he first loved us. That is a reorientation of the soul that only can come to us when the Spirit of God does his deep work.

The Story of Joseph

The symbol of Joseph's life is the coat of many different colors. He received this coat from his father, Jacob, who loved him more than he loved any of his other children. He was the first son born to his wife, Rachel, whom he loved deeply. There is so much irony in the story of Joseph because as the favorite son who was bestowed so much affection and favoritism, this same son would experience incredible rejection in his life. There are so many levels of understanding the life of Joseph that could be expressed, including the truth that Joseph was indeed a type that foreshadowed Christ. He was rejected by men, placed in the ground for three days, sold out for twenty pieces of silver, left Canaan for Egypt, and was rewarded with a kingdom. But that is not the thrust of the story that we want to discover.

The story of Joseph was one of a father who loved him deeply, yet he experienced rejection and disappointment in people all around him. Jacob kept
his son close to him at home while the rest of his sons were working the fields
with the sheep. It was clear to his brothers that Joseph had the heart of the
father. Usually, the oldest would receive the greatest attention, or even the
youngest. But in this case, it was Joseph. The coat was a constant reminder
that the father's affection was his above all the others.

Joseph didn't help himself when God revealed his future with dreams.
Rather than keep these things to himself and ponder them, he decided to
tell all his brothers. The dreams contained images that would infuriate his
siblings. In the first dream, he boasted about how they were tying up sheaves
of grain, and his sheave rose up, and all their sheaves bowed down to his. In
the second dream, he saw the sun, moon, and eleven stars bowing down to
him. In each case, he drew the ire of his family. They questioned his sanity as
they asked, "Do you intend to reign over us? Will you actually rule us?" (Gen.
37:8). Even his father rebuked him when he heard about the sun and the
moon bowing down because he recognized that he was represented by the sun.

It wasn't long before the jealousy of the brothers resulted in Joseph being
completely rejected and thrown into an empty cistern. If it wasn't for his one
brother Reuben, they would have killed him then and there. Imagine the extent of the rejection of your family, being left for dead in a hole in the ground.
But God had other plans for Joseph, and just at the right moment, a caravan
of Ishmaelite's came, which triggered Judah's desire to make some money by
selling off his brother as a slave.

Life can become disorienting at times. Imagine what was going on in the
soul of Joseph. His entire life up to that point was being a favored son who
would do anything for him. Then, suddenly, you find yourself sold into slavery
by your own brothers. Now that is disorienting to the soul! He must asked
himself a thousand times how he got to where he now was—a slave traveling with strangers, with a destiny uncertain but surely without promise. His
orientation of God was full acceptance and affection. But now that premise
would be challenged. That is what disorientation does to us. It challenges our
understanding of God and how we related to him. If God loves me, how can
He allow this to happen to me? What about God's covenant of love given to
my forefathers, Abraham and Jacob?

The life of Joseph was filled with rejection. His brothers were only the first
in line. God was indeed watching over Joseph and guiding his life, but not
the way Joseph would have planned it. He found himself being owned by Potiphar, a trusted official of Pharaoh. God gave Joseph success in everything he
did, and it was noticed. So much so that Potiphar gave Joseph responsibility

to care for everything that was his. But it wasn't long before blessing would result in rejection. Potiphar's wife desired to have Joseph, and when he refused, it landed him in prison. He was unjustly accused of trying to rape Potiphar's wife as she hated Joseph for refusing her advances.

Unjust suffering is hard to take. Rejection without cause is disorienting. Jesus understood, for he hung on the cross not for our sins but for the sins of the world. Jesus had the love of the Father, but he also suffered unjustly but willingly. Most of us, though, find suffering unjust or rejection very disorienting. Our souls long to be loved and accepted. Somehow, we know that God created our souls for love, and something is wrong. We strive for acceptance. We want others to care. The soul is hungry for it.

I have a friend who was woken up in the middle of the night and taken away in handcuffs and charged with racketeering. This man had outstanding character and was an active elder in the church. He was known by everyone as someone who would go out of his way to help you. He found himself wondering what he did to deserve being arrested and facing twenty-five years in jail, which pretty much was a life sentence because of his age. He had done nothing but dealt honorably in all of his transactions as a businessman. What he didn't know was that some of his clients were not so upright and had used him to cover their own sinful ways. The shame and pain of being treated like a criminal was disorienting to his soul. He cried out day and night for God to vindicate him. It has been more than two years of crying out to God for help without an answer—or at least an answer that he is looking for. He refused to plead guilty to receive a lighter sentence because he was innocent. The FBI however continues relentlessly to destroy his life. More than two years later, the case has yet to be tried, and no settlement has been agreed upon. Imagine what is happening in his soul as he ponders the disorientation of his soul.

We frequently talk about what is going on in his soul through all of this. What he shares is truly amazing. He said the whole experience has been like hell. The feelings of rejection, questioning of oneself, the would-have and should-haves race through his head—all are torturous. However, he says he has grown to understand the love of God so much more through the experience. His intimacy with Christ has deepened beyond any time in his life.

In times of disorientation, we can become bitter or we can draw closer to Christ. In the story of Joseph, we never read about Joseph growing bitter. It appears that he grew stronger in his faith and the covenantal care of Yahweh. Disappointment continued when he interpreted the dream of the baker and the cupbearer accurately. He was promised by the cupbearer that he would bring up his case to the supreme ruler of the land, but the cupbearer forgot. He rotted in prison longer.

Waiting is disorienting to the soul. Waiting on God to demonstrate his care can feel like rejection. The soul is tempted to question the nature of God's love. But in the waiting, it may be that God is at work in ways we don't understand at the moment. That is where he does the greatest soul work. That is where disciples grow. This is what happened to Joseph. He did not let his soul be shaped by the rejection of his brothers, Potiphar's wife, the failure of the cupbearer to remember him, but rather by the love of God.

Don't miss understand. Joseph experienced pain. Rejection is painful because love accepts. Love embraces and cares. When his brothers come to Egypt later in the story to obtain grain during the famine, Joseph is now ruling over Egypt according to the sovereign plan of God that was being orchestrated. You see, God did care. Not just about Joseph, but about his entire family. When he saw his brothers and recognized them, he could hardly bear the pain and had to leave the room. But that pain was turned into joy. The process of orientation, disorientation, and reorientation was now complete. Joseph understood that what his brothers had done to him was meant for evil, but God used it for good (Gen. 50:20).

We don't always have the end of the story to reconcile our souls with what God is doing. We often just have the promise of Scripture, which tells us "that in all things God works for the good of those who love him, who have been called according to his purpose" (Rom. 8:28). We also have the knowledge that Christ died for us. This is the most reorienting truth of Scripture.

The process of discipleship includes the processing of life through the stages of orientation–disorientation–and reorientation. As disciplers, we have the opportunity to help others along this journey. It is in the community of faith that the Spirit of God so often speaks with clarity. We must not forsake the gathering together of the saints, for we need one another. We are members of one body.

Reflection Questions

1. The life of discipleship is likened to that of a blacksmith who molds iron. It is a painful and violent process. What has your experience of discipleship been like?

2. Describe the greatest moments of spiritual growth and discipleship in your life. How do they relate to the three stories of Job, Solomon, and Joseph?

3. Where are you currently? Are you in orientation, disorientation, or reorientation?

4. How can you use the concepts in this chapter to help you disciple others?

21

Deep Repentance

*They will come back shedding tears of contrition. I will
bring them back praying prayers of repentance. I will
lead them besides streams of water, along smooth paths
where they will never stumble. I will do this because I
am Israel's father; Ephraim is my firstborn son.*

—Jeremiah 39:9

W hen I met Jonathan, he was a broken man. After hearing the Gospel
of God's grace and love, he completely melted down in a waterfall of
tears. The love of Christ would change him...not once but many times. He
is still being changed.

Jonathan's father died when he was very young. In fact, he had no recol-
lection of his own father. His mother did her best to raise her son without a
father but soon collapsed under the pressure. She was diagnosed and hospital-
ized with schizophrenia. The only people in Jonathan's life who was willing
to take him in were his grandparents. They did their best to parent this child,
but they were old and not in good health. Truth be told, they were inadequate. Jonathan's life was imprinted with mistrust, pain, and instability. He
had to fight to be relevant to the world. He usually lost. His demeanor proved
to anyone who met him that he was afraid, defeated, and desperate. But God

changed all of that! Life for Jonathan would change direction. It began with repentance. It continues with repentance.

John the Baptist preached a message of repentance in anticipation and preparation for salvation and the appearance of the Messiah (John 1). Jesus declared, "Repent for the Kingdom of God is near" (Matt. 4:17). The apostles also called people to repentance and to turn away from their sins (Acts 3:19). Repentance is necessary to follow Christ and critical in the receiving of the Gospel of grace.

Repentance (metanoia) is a rich word in the Scriptures. In ancient Greek literature, the word had no moral content but simply means to change your mind about something. The word could just as much denote a change of mind to go and murder someone instead of forgiving him.[43] But in Scripture, the word was further developed. It still carried with it the idea of changing one's mind about something, but it was deeper and more profound. Understanding metanoia is key to discipleship.

> We can no longer be satisfied with a surface repentance that leaves the person unchanged. We must go after the deep-soul repentance that is transformational.

Metanoia is used to describe not just a change of mind but a conversion of life. Jesus said, "Repent, and turn from your sins, so that your sins will be wiped out" (Matt. 3:17, ESV). Acts 20:21 records for us that both Jews and Gentiles were being called to metanoia and place their faith in Christ and follow him. The idea is richer than simply changing one's mind. Metanoia was the precursor to a change of direction of one's life.

Metanoia in the writings of Paul expands the use of the word to be accompanied by sorrow. Sin is rebellion toward God's kingdom and results in pain for both the one sinning and the impact of that sin on the world. Paul says, "As it is, I rejoice, not because you were grieved, but because you were grieved into repenting. For you felt a godly grief, so that you suffered no loss through us" (1 Cor 7:9). Sorrow and grief precede the change of life. So metanoia includes both a change of mind and a corresponding impact on the emotional core of our being. There is a regret for the destructive nature of the sin. There is a keen sense of awareness of the power and pain of not living for the kingdom of God.

It should also be pointed out that metanoia or repentance is not something that is only needed and necessary at conversion. Paul calls for a continual metanoia in the believer's life. Paul was writing to the Corinthian church, which had experienced conversion but were not living life in accordance with the conversion of their souls. John warns the early church that if repentance (metanoia) does not ensue, the lampstand would be removed from the church of Ephesus (Rev. 2:5). Repentance is the means by which the follower of Christ grows in sanctification by the Spirit of God. Repentance should be a regular, daily process of aligning oneself with Christ and his kingdom.

The Scripture teaches us that repentance is experienced at different levels. Let me see if I can unpack them in a way that will motivate us to go after a deep repentance. We can no longer be satisfied with a surface repentance that leaves the person unchanged. We must go after a deep-soul repentance that is transformational.

The core teaching on different kinds of repentance comes from Paul's teaching in 1 Corinthians 7 but is sprinkled throughout the Scriptures, both the Old Testament and New Testament. Here is this pivotal teaching of Paul:

> I rejoice, not because you were grieved, but because you were grieved into repenting. For you felt a godly grief, so that you suffered no loss through us. For godly grief produces a repentance that leads to salvation without regret, whereas worldly grief produces death. For see what earnestness this godly grief has produced in you, but also what eagerness to clear yourselves, what indignation, what fear, what longing, what zeal, what punishment! (1 Cor. 7:9–11)

For many years, I was taught that metanoia simply meant "to change your mind." I swallowed that partial "truth." These teachers were godly men who wanted to preserve the grace of God. For these teachers, to believe that repentance involved feelings and behavior change was dangerous. It came too close to tying salvation to works. They wanted to protect the Gospel of grace that was separate from men's works. This resulted in teaching that was disconnected from the rest of Scripture. It resulted in a cheap grace because repentance was divorced from the soul of man. Actually, it is not repentance at all! To make matters worse, the change of mind wasn't very deep in understanding, either.

Here are levels of repentance offered in Scripture:

1. A change of mind about truth
2. A change of mind that is accompanied by grief and sorrow that leads to death
3. A change of mind that is accompanied by grief and sorrow that leads to life

4. A change of mind that is accompanied by grief and sorrow that leads to life and breaks the power of sin

A change of mind about truth. I don't think we need to say too much about this partial truth. Salvation is found in Christ alone. We must believe that he is the source of our salvation and believe his Gospel. However, as James states, "Even the demons believe and shutter" (James 2:19). James points out the error of thinking that true repentance is a matter of believing or not believing in facts about God, or having good theology. James points out that demons have great theology and even get the Trinity right.

Initially, when Jonathan responded to the Gospel, he had very clear change of mind about many things on God. He believed in the God of grace and that Jesus was offering forgiveness of sin. He even prayed a prayer of salvation and began his journey as a follower of Christ. There was no doubt about his change of thinking on how forgiveness is obtained—only through the work of Christ on the cross.

A change of mind that is accompanied by grief and sorrow that leads to death. Paul adds more to understanding repentance by discussing the role of grief and sorrow. Grief is the emotion we feel when there is a loss. Sorrow is something we feel when something bad has happened to us. Certainly, grief and sorrow are a part of a life lived in sin. But he indicates that both do not necessarily lead to life. There is a kind of grief and sorrow that leads to death. We can agree with the truth of the Gospel, have grief and sorrow, and still not have repentance that leads to life. We can grieve the penalties of sin and be sorry that we have committed it because the consequences are awful and destructive.

For Jonathan, he was tied into a destructive life of homosexuality and pornography. He wrestled with the sin because it caused him so many problems. Initially, his turning to Christ was the result of a breakup with a man whom he was living. He was looking for relief from the consequences of his sin.

A change of mind that is accompanied by grief and sorrow that leads to life. All grief and sorrow are not the same. The kind of grief and sorrow that Paul is speaking about is grief about the offense of sin to a holy loving God. The object of grief is not self but rather God himself. He is not sorry that he has experienced pain and grief, and he is not trying to merely escape the wrath of God but is grieving how his own sin has separated him from God's love. He understands the nature of sin and is hungering for God. This level of repentance begins to hate not just the consequence of sin but the sin itself. He wants to avoid the sin that he has been in bondage to and is in chains.

Jonathan came to this point in his own life one Sunday morning while driving to church. By this time, he was married and had a child. He loved them both dearly. However, he was still caught up in his sin. It was secret. Secret sin is always the most powerful. True repentance brings what is in darkness out into the light. 1 John 1:5–9 connects repentance with living in the light,

> This is the message we have heard from him and declare to you: God is light; in him there is no darkness at all. If we claim to have fellowship with him and yet walk in the darkness, we lie and do not live out the truth. But if we walk in the light, as he is in the light, we have fellowship with one another, and the blood of Jesus, his Son, purifies us from all sin. If we claim to be without sin, we deceive ourselves and the truth is not in us. If we confess our sins, he is faithful and just and will forgive us our sins and purify us from all unrighteousness.

While driving to church with his family, he was actually on the cell phone having phone sex. He hated what he was doing and felt like a hypocrite. But he also loved his sin. He was in agreement with Christ about grace and sin and felt sorrow for what sin was doing to him and his family. Sin still gripped him. That very day, he took his sin out of the darkness and into the light. He confessed the sin with his mouth to his wife and pastor. He even confessed his sin to his small group in great detail. His life was filthy. He was seeing prostitutes, and the pornography that he was introduced to by his grandfather at an early age had held him in bondage and had grown to an addiction. Jonathan shared openly and received grace from God, and so much changed that day for him and his family. There was godly sorrow and grief. He saw the awful nature of his sin and was drawn to God in a new way. His love for God was evident to everyone.

When I think about Jonathan, I can't help but think of the woman in Luke 7 who came to the house of the Pharisee Simon and fell at Jesus's feet and began washing them with her alabaster jar of perfume. Simon was disgusted about what was happening, for he knew that this was a "sinful" woman (prostitute) who was touching Jesus. Jesus then told a parable about two men who owed money to a banker and were both forgiven. One owed a little and other owed much. Jesus then asked Simon, "Who do you think loved more?" Clearly, the man who was forgiven much loved more. That is Jonathan. He knows how much he was forgiven, and it has changed his life. It changed his love. Discipleship is about growing in our love for the Savior.

A change of mind that is accompanied by grief and sorrow that leads to life and breaks the power of sin. The story of Jonathan is not yet finished. He has stopped the pattern of sin in his life, and he is experiencing greater intimacy with Christ. But could there be a deeper kind of repentance? I believe so.

Jonathan is growing in his love for Jesus and his heavenly Father. But I am not sure that Jonathan has come to grips with what was fueling his sinful life. Oftentimes, we stop with repenting our sin, but we haven't gone deeper in understanding what is driving our sin and addiction to sinful behavior? What if we would identify the motivation of our sin and repent at that deeper level? What if we actually repented on the "why" as well as the "what"?

If we were created for love that only God can satisfy, apart from the love of God, our souls will pursue that emptiness in sinful ways. We know that love is experienced in three spheres: acceptance, significance, and security. We tend to strive after love apart from God, using things that were never intended to fill that hole in our souls. When we latch onto these substitutes and count on them (form our identities around them), they become "inordinate attachments" that we need to be freed. Soul discipleship requires identifying and going after these attachments because these keep us from being free from the power of sin. Ultimately, this is a work of the Spirit. Only the Spirit of God can free us, as we yield to his work in our lives. As disciplers, we must help people identify the power of sin that lurks under the surface. This will require not just repentance of sin but repentance of what is driving sin.

Jonathan's soul has an inordinate attachment for acceptance. He doesn't fit in. He never has. He thought if he was married, he would be accepted. Then he thought if he had a child, he would know the acceptance he was striving after. Neither satisfied the insatiable need for acceptance. Acceptance includes the need for intimacy, care, and belonging. Oftentimes men turn to sexuality to meet this need in their lives. Until Jonathan repents more deeply, not just about his presenting sin, but what is driving the sin underneath, he will be vulnerable to the attack of Satan. Only Christ can provide the love and intimacy that he is desperate to know. Only in Christ is it guaranteed and dependable. Repentance about where he finds his identity is what is needed. It is the love of God that changes us. Remember, the Spirit of God is witnessing to our spirit that we are sons of God. Only sons know the love of the Father that undergirds all of life.

The lack of repentance at this deeper level puts a lid on our sanctification in this life. The truth is that repentance over actual sins, without going deeper in repenting about what is driving the sin, is only temporary. If the soul is not transformed, we are only doing behavior modification. A sinful soul (one that is pursuing life through anything apart from Christ) will be exposed when whatever is filling the hole is removed. Some pursue significance through performance. Others strive after safety through control and manipulation. We all are susceptible to the temptations of Satan when our attachments are outside of Christ.

Why is Christian maturity so elusive? Why do Christian leaders disappoint so often? I believe it is related to our failure to go deeper into repentance. Our soul is not matured. We have confessed our sinful acts but have left the weightier issue of what is driving that sinful behavior untouched. The old illustration about the toothpaste and the toothpaste tube is true. When you squeeze the tube, whatever is inside comes out. If the soul has never been cleansed, all kinds of dirt and filth is revealed. Perhaps we should consider the words of Christ and clean the inside of the cup rather than just cleaning the outside of the cup. If you clean the inside, the outside is clean already.

How we gain our identity (acceptance, significance, and security) determines to a great extent how we will live our lives. Our identity and need for love is not optional in our lives, but that which we must have to live. The formation of our identity "in Christ" is paramount. It is the essence of soul discipleship. And this is the very approach to discipleship that we find in Scripture. This is why we find Paul speaking about being "in Christ" more than ninety times. It is because we are "in Christ" and "Christ is in us" that we can live a sanctified life. Our identity changed when we were saved. Paul says, "Therefore, if anyone is in Christ, he is a new creation. The old has passed away; behold, the new has come" (2 Cor. 5:17). There is a new creation, a new life, a newborn reality that defines our life. We are sons of God now. That changes everything!

Paul is instructing the church how to live out the faith by tying everything they do to their new identity. He even asks this important question at the end of 2 Corinthians: "Or do you not realize this about yourselves, that Jesus Christ is in you?" (2 Cor. 13:5). His logic is that if you have clarity on your identity, then you would be living out that identity. Paul links everything about discipleship to identity: our being chosen, predestined, sealed, redeemed, washed of sin, forgiven of sin, our unity in the body, sonship, every spiritual blessing, our power, our testimony, our ministry of reconciliation, wisdom, his kindness, our work, intimacy, his dwelling in us, our freedom and confidence. Just read through Ephesians and underline the number of times Paul refers to our identity being "in Christ." You will be amazed.

I know much is made in today's world about modeling as the primary means of discipleship. We often quote Paul, "Follow my example as I follow the example of Christ" (1 Cor. 11:1). F. F. Bruce wrote a classic book about the making of disciples, which is insightful and exhaustive but really doesn't get into the issues of the soul.[44] Some speak about the Talmud way of making disciples, like the Jewish rabbi did in the time of Christ. The disciples walked

so close to the rabbi that the dust of the rabbi got on the dust of their san-
dals. The principle being emphasized again is the idea of modeling. I am not
denying that modeling and imitation is a great teaching tool, but I wonder if
we neglect the soul issues in favor of methodology. Didn't Jesus teach about
the soul and challenged what is going on in the soul? In the process of the
disciples watching the life of Christ, they were constantly being challenged
about what was going on in their souls. For example, when the disciples were
arguing about who would be the greatest, Jesus went for the soul. What drives
man to want to lord over others? Perhaps Jesus was getting at the drive for
significance in his teaching. The way of significance is to be a servant. He
modeled servanthood, and he also confronted the soul's evil desire.

The Pharisees actually used the approach of modeling and used it as a
hammer. They criticized anyone who didn't do what they did, even Jesus!
The Gospel of Mark in chapter 7 records the story:

> Now when the Pharisees gathered to him, with some of the scribes who
> had come from Jerusalem, they saw that some of his disciples ate with
> hands that were defiled, that is, unwashed. (For the Pharisees and all the
> Jews do not eat unless they wash their hands properly, holding to the tra-
> dition of the elders, and when they come from the marketplace, they do
> not eat unless they wash. And there are many other traditions that they
> observe, such as the washing of cups and pots and copper vessels and
> dining couches.) And the Pharisees and the scribes asked him, "Why do
> your disciples not walk according to the tradition of the elders, but eat
> with defiled hands?" And he said to them, "Well did Isaiah prophesy of
> you hypocrites, as it is written,
>
> "'This people honors me with their lips,
>   but their heart is far from me;
>   in vain do they worship me,
>   teaching as doctrines the commandments of men.'
> You leave the commandment of God and hold to the tradition of men."

The method of modeling can be powerful. It kept the nation of Israel in
bondage for four hundred years. The consistent modeling of pharisaical Ju-
daism was successful in producing fruit after its own kind. The problem with
modeling is that unless the person modeling is living the life of Christ, it can
simply be another form of religiosity rather than a transformation of the soul.
Notice that Jesus responds to the Pharisees by going after the heart (soul).
Jesus was concerned about where their heart was, not how they washed their

hands. If modeling is our methodology, we must learn to do like Jesus and have soul conversations as well. The soul needs discipling. Not just behavior change.

I am not so concerned with the methodology of modeling. I just believe that modeling certain behavior is not going to get the job done. The real question is whether or not we actually get to the issues of the soul. Perhaps if we have people who have been soul-transformed, living in such a way that it causes deep conversation with disciples about soul issues, that would make a big difference. If the focus of our modeling is on behavior, and our content of teaching is about outward conformity to living moral lives, I'm afraid that we will make little progress in the making of disciples who live like Paul and the apostles.

Reflection Questions

1. Stubborn sin and recurring sin is common in the life of the church. Jonathan found a way out. What was his secret, and how can we help others find an escape?

2. Repentance according to Scripture can be done at different levels. Identify the four levels and discuss the level of repentance that you have experienced.

3. How is your discipleship process focused on identity ("in Christ")? How can your approach be more directed at the soul and identity going forward?

4. How can we go deeper in our repentance, and how can we help others go deeper into repentance?

22

The Key to Freedom

It is for freedom that Christ has set us free.

—Galatians 5:1

We all want to be free. We don't like to be controlled or manipulated. Slavery is the symbol of being defeated. In the first real job I had in high school, I was helping rip a roof off a building. There were layers of shingles several inches thick. It was a brutally hot summer's day, so sweat was

> *It is possible to be free and live in bondage.*

pouring off my face, and it made it difficult for me to see. When I got down to the wood sheathing, I could see that it was rotted. Actually, I put my foot through the roof. Peering into the hole, the sunlight put a spotlight on a set of chains that were fixed to the wall. I had just opened an attic that hadn't seen the light of day in more than a century. The building was almost three hundred years old. After tearing off all the rotted boards, I could clearly see two sets of chains with shackles, as well as an iron poker-type tool with a sharp point on the end. A historian was called in to examine what was found, and it was determined that slaves had once been regularly shackled in this attic. The discovery was taken and placed in a sealed frame and hangs as a display with the history of this historic site. I can't imagine having those heavy chains on my hands and feet. Yet this is exactly how most people live spiritually. We may not have full awareness that we are shackled, but that is our reality.

Paul makes this promise about the Christ life: "You, my brothers and sisters, were called to be free" (Gal. 5:13). Then he goes on to give us the key to freedom. He warns us that freedom is not doing anything you desire in the flesh. In actuality, that is really bondage. Your fleshly nature is like a set of chains around your wrists and ankles. You are controlled by your flesh. It is your passions and desires that hold you in captivity (Gal. 5:24). It is those passions and desires that you believe will satisfy and give you life. If only I had ——, then I would be satisfied. Our lives are spent looking to fill the hole in our soul—"Accept me," "Look at me," "I'm important," "I need a bigger savings account so I can feel safe," "Look what I did," "See what I have?" The striving to fill the hole in our heart is an attempt to replace that which we don't know—the love of God.

> **We don't live generously when we have unmet needs of our own.**

Galatians chapter 5 gives us the key to living in freedom. In Christ, we are set free. Sin has no power over us. Christ paid the penalty for our sin, and we were set free from the power of sin. Paul warns us then not to use our freedom foolishly. It is possible to be free and live in bondage. Unfortunately, this is the testimony of many believers. There is limited experience of the kind of freedom God offers us. The key is love.

The Gospel is about the love of God freely given. Yet our pattern of life is to strive after love rather than to receive it. This results in selfish living. Paul warns us, "If you bite and devour each other, watch out or you will be destroyed by each other" (Gal. 5:15). Why is the church often a place of turmoil and fighting? Because we have yet to understand in our souls the love of God. We can't love each other because we are too busy trying to attain love. It consumes us. We really are in bondage. We demand that we be loved by others, and we are easily offended when that love is not felt and experienced.

Paul draws a contrast between what is often the case and what life should be for the disciple of Christ: "But do not use your freedom to indulge the flesh; rather, serve one another humbly in love. For the entire law is fulfilled in keeping this one command; 'Love your neighbor as yourself'" (Gal. 5:13–14). Why is this command to humble ourselves and love others so difficult? It is because we have a void in our souls in grasping the love of God that is freely given. We just don't get it. We are already accepted, significant, and secure in

Christ. But we use all our energy and efforts to strive after love from other sources, including our brothers and sisters in Christ. We cannot love our neighbors when we have a need in our own heart that is not filled. It is like a neighbor asking you to give them a million-dollar loan when you are bankrupt or have just enough for yourself. You have nothing to offer. You yourself are looking for someone to give you money! That is our state when we fail to understand the fullness of God's love. We don't live generously when we have unmet needs of our own.

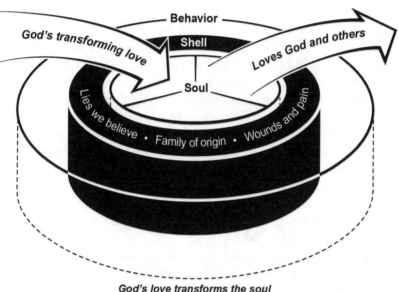

God's love transforms the soul
No longer motivated/controlled by a need to generate love for oneself.

Paul points us to an alternative, and that is to live according to the Spirit of God. Remember, the Spirit of God teaches us that we are fully loved sons of God (Rom. 8:15–17). We are not slaves (same metaphor). Sons are not orphans or slaves who have to strive after love. The love of the Father transforms them. Their souls are full of God's love. They know how to love because they know the love of the Father. Discipleship must remind people and help them to understand the love of the Father.

At this point in the book, perhaps you may feel that this idea of love is getting repetitive. That is intentional. That is the teaching of Scripture. Let's not get tired of talking about the love of God! We never move on from growing in the love of God. His love is infinite. Nothing transforms like the love of God as we experience it in Christ.

The love of God is what allows us to risk everything for him. I cannot think of a safer place to be than under the love of God. Obedience is not scary even if it is dangerous. I can risk losing a friend if I am rejected by my neighbor for sharing about my love of Christ. David knew God's love and stood up to Goliath. Daniel faced the lions. You can face your neighbor or that coworker. Yet our experience with God's love when limited puts us back in chains. My mouth is sealed shut. What if? How can we trust a God who may not protect us? How can I join God in his mission to reconcile the world to himself if I am on my own mission to fill my own soul with substitutes for God's love? I can't. I won't.

The average Christian in the United States will spend more on coffee than on support of the mission of Christ to those who have never heard about God's love and his provision through Christ. The church has tried to fix this problem with stewardship training, guilt, greater vision, fund-raising campaigns, etc., without much gain. In fact, the church is giving less and less to the advancement of the kingdom in the darkest places (as a percentage of income). We have a love problem. If we understood the love of God, we would be full. God's love would be running out of us and into the world. Then and only then will we do as Christ taught and Paul taught: "Love your neighbor as yourself." I like this saying of G. K. Chesterton: "The Bible tells us to love our neighbors, and also to love our enemies; probably because they are generally the same people."[45] It is only the supernatural love of God in us that will enable us to love others.

When we know the love of God and his presence, so much takes place as a result. True freedom is released. We become thankful rather than "grabful." God's love produces a heart of thanksgiving. We are full. We don't need anything more, so our demanding spirit ceases. The chains fall off. Freedom.

A soul that is experiencing the fullness of the love of God results in thanksgiving. A thankful heart results in a life of joy. The psalmist wrote, "And let them offer sacrifices of thanksgiving, and tell of his deeds in songs of joy!" (Ps. 107:22). Joy always accompanies thanksgiving. The soul is full and rejoices. It is generous in pouring out love on others. Grace received begets gratefulness in the heart. A grateful heart begets a life of joy.

Lauren Suval discusses the connection between thanksgiving and joy in her blog: "Dennis Prager, author of Happiness is a Serious Problem, discusses gratitude in his book as the secret to being happy. However, he believes expectations undermine gratitude and therefore undermine happiness. 'The more expectations you have, the less gratitude you will have. If you get what you expect, you will not be grateful for getting it.'"[46] He suggests lowering expectations, particularly pertaining to circumstances beyond your control, in order to bring gratitude to fruition. Dennis Prager acknowledges that thanksgiving and joy are connected. However, he also notes that when a person has high expectations, they will not have as much thanksgiving because they become disappointed. His answer is to lower expectations. Although I get his point, there is another solution. Rather than lowering our expectations in life, perhaps we should direct our thanksgiving more toward the God who loves us and from whom we have life. Disappointment is part of life because of sin and its destructive nature. The only constant that we can depend on is God's love over us. That never disappoints. The Gospel is the source of our thanksgiving and our joy.

God laid a burden on the heart of Nehemiah for Jerusalem, and he risked going to the king. Israel was in exile, and the walls of Jerusalem had been knocked down. God moved the heart of the king to enable Nehemiah to go and rebuild the walls. When it was completed and the people began to resettle behind the safety of the walls, there was a great convocation of the people where Ezra read the Word of God to the people. It was a day for great thanksgiving. Nehemiah instructed the nation not to grieve but to rejoice. This was a day of thanksgiving and rejoicing. He said, "The joy of the LORD is our strength." We are strong when we are rejoicing in the Lord our God. We are weak when we fail to rejoice. Our souls fail and give up.

What if God's people were discipled in the incredible love of God that has its source in the work of Christ on the cross? What if we discipled the soul to find its orientation in that same great love? Is it possible that the church of Christ would rise up in thanksgiving and in the fullness of joy with great strength? The absence of joy in the church is telling. It reveals a searching for acceptance, significance, and security in something other than the precious love of God. But I have hope that we will once again return to the simple Gospel—God so loved the world that he gave his only Son.

By now, you have learned that my approach to the Christian life is grounded in the love of God. Not everyone takes this approach. I would like to make some reflections on a couple of approaches to the Christian life that are popular today but will have a limited shelf life. They have an appeal and a great following. They also are not far away from what we have been discussing in this book. However, they are not organizational and foundational, and you can't build upon them. I don't claim to be above those who propose them, nor am I anyone's final authority. I simply make some reflections on what I have learned and continue to learn in the process of living out discipleship. *Missional*

Many people today have proposed that discipleship be oriented around being missional. There is much that I like about this movement, and to be honest, I have counted myself as someone who has championed the missional movement. As a district superintendent leading a district of churches and pastors, I have brought in speakers, distributed books, and raised up "missional churches." I am attracted to the emphasis on going into the world and not living behind the fortress of the church walls. I know that when we are on mission, we are stretched in our faith and learn to depend on his Spirit. I also believe we serve a missional God—One who has as his mission to redeem the world. I love parties! Jesus did too. He didn't come to condemn people but to rescue them from their sin. We should not be afraid of being contaminated by the world. I am also for intentional discipleship, which multiplies itself over and over again. This has been part of what I have embraced in the missional movement.

> *The fuel for mission is not organizing all the teaching around the mission but organizing our mission around the gospel.*

Well then, why am I critical about organizing the Christian life around being missional? The simple reason is that putting forth mission as the organizational principle is putting the cart before the horse. You can't drive missional work until your soul has been transformed by the love of God. Love drives the mission. Missionality is the result of a soul filled with God's love that spills over into the world.

Six years ago, I joined a church plant that would structure itself around the concepts of the missional church. As most people know, those who have tried to structure a church around being missional, it is a difficult and slow way to build a church. Instead of trying to attract people to a service, the mission is to live out the life of Christ in the world. This sounds great on paper. It is another thing to implement in a community of faith. What we discovered is that most of the missional living that was taking place was really being done by the pastors of the church. Yes, a few more joined in and began the risky behavior, but overall, the church found the concepts foreign and dangerous. People enjoyed the preaching on missional living and celebrated the new life that was being born into the church by God's grace, but participation was an uphill battle. *Battle* is the right word to describe it. What we learned is that the fuel for mission is not organizing all the teaching around the mission but organizing our lives around the Gospel—God so loved the world. Until the hard work of orientation, disorientation, reorientation of the soul takes place, being a missional church is like pushing a train uphill. Even a small stick on the tracks can stop the momentum.

I do believe that the fruit of the Gospel in one's soul is a missional lifestyle. I am also not opposed to using the word *missional* and teaching missional principles, but we must get the cart behind the horse. If you don't, you will have no choice but to drive the sheep into submission. The force for mission must be inside them, not just outside. People may fake it for a time or do just enough to give you hope and believe you are making progress, but when you stop checking in and holding them accountable, they will return to filling their own heart for it is empty and desperate. Only a soul that is overflowing will live that way.

Another movement that I have concern with is those who attempt to organize life around the kingdom. Actually, I embraced much of kingdom theology when it was being developed under Gordon Ladd. It certainly helped me to better understand the fullness of the Gospel and the mission of God with greater breath. It also formed some of my eschatology. One of the most valuable experiences in seminary for me was reading through the Gospels and underlining everything in purple that referred to the mission and kingdom of Christ. If we can join Christ in his mission, which is defined as "kingdom," we would certainly be on track.

Books like *The Hole in Our Gospel* by Richard Stearns[47] filled in things that were missing in my narrower view of the Gospel. No one can argue that when Jesus introduced himself publically in his mission, he quoted from Isaiah 61. God has as his mission to bring about justice and right wrongs. He is about healing and restoration, not just of the soul but also our physical being. God is not just saving souls; he is saving the cosmos.

This generation is responding to this call to establish the kingdom of God on earth. They are passionate about justice and are willing, at least to some degree, to suffer along with those who are marginalized and to stand with them. This message also resonates with the unregenerate. The world wants what Christ came to do. This is all good and right.

But the same problem exists with the kingdom movement as with the missional movement. Neither of them can be sustained without the foundation of God's love filling the soul. I have spoken to young pastors who get discouraged because they plan an event to address an issue of injustice or to clean up a river or serve the poor, and very few people actually show up. Because the organizing principle for them is that we must join God in his work in the world, they double down on that message in preaching and in their discipleship. When there is a response of a few, they are championed and made heroes, but that only serves to turn off those who didn't participate as they feel badly. Guilt is a poor motivator of righteous living. It is the kindness of God that leads us to repentance. If the leader is driven to succeed (his own heart needs significance from what he is doing), he may go down the road of browbeating or manipulation.

If a person's soul is full and running over with the love of God, you will have an engine to drive the mission and the work of the kingdom. Otherwise, you will find yourself pushing that train uphill. It doesn't matter how many people you have pushing; you will get tired and give up. When the mission is driven by the love of God and the power of the Spirit from within, God does a mighty and sustainable work. Let us be people who build our discipleship movement in the soul that can power the mission and kingdom work of our Savior.

Reflection Questions

1. How is living generously linked to the love of God and the passions of the soul?

2. We are called as disciples to be on mission with Christ. However, very few people are engaged in both local and worldwide mission with any passion or sacrifice. Why do you think this is? How can we disciple people's soul that would result in a change in motivation?

3. Can a "missional church" or church focused on the "kingdom of God" be sustained without discipling the soul? Why or why not?

23

Physician of the Soul Training

And Jesus came and said to them, "All authority in heaven and on earth has been given to me. Go therefore and make disciples of all nations, baptizing them in[a] the name of the Father and of the Son and of the Holy Spirit, teaching them to observe all that I have commanded you. And behold, I am with you always, to the end of the age."

—Matthew 28:18–20

The making of disciples is the call of all those who have received the Gospel and are followers of Christ. It is the means by which people are deeply transformed to love like God loves. Outside the cup, discipleship that focuses on behavior and conformity to rules and morality cannot succeed in producing righteousness. Jesus is our Savior. Apart from his regenerating work accomplished on the cross, we are lost and without hope. We declare and celebrate this moving from death to life in the picture of baptism (Rom. 6:1–14). But Jesus is also our Sanctifier. He saves us from our sin and calls us his sons and daughters. God's unconditional love changes our soul. And in God's infinite wisdom, he has called his disciples to participate in this process

197

of making disciples who conform to the image of Christ. The work of discipleship is essentially soul work, for whatever is on the inside is what determines how we live on the outside.

This author is calling out the church to not only understand the role of the soul in disciple making but to equip the saints to be physicians of the soul. Most Christians today are ignorant of the anatomy of the soul and how the soul controls the life of a person. What if the church was committed to equipping every disciple to be a physician of the soul and would release them not to programs but to make disciples? I am not saying that programs can't be used by God to make disciples. What I am saying is that there is little emphasis on equipping the saints to do soul work.

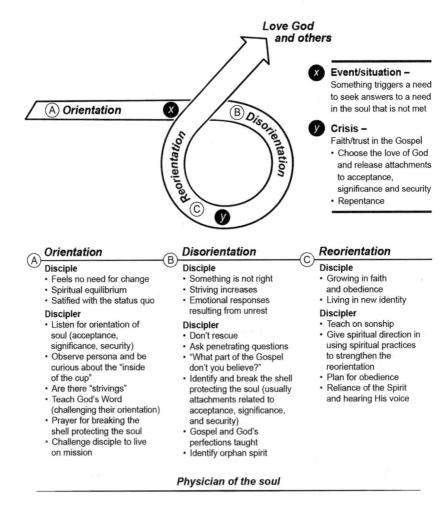

Love God and others

x Event/situation –
Something triggers a need to seek answers to a need in the soul that is not met

y Crisis –
Faith/trust in the Gospel
• Choose the love of God and release attachments to acceptance, significance and security
• Repentance

(A) **Orientation**	(B) **Disorientation**	(C) **Reorientation**
Disciple	**Disciple**	**Disciple**
• Feels no need for change	• Something is not right	• Growing in faith and obedience
• Spiritual equilibrium	• Striving increases	• Living in new identity
• Satified with the status quo	• Emotional responses resulting from unrest	**Discipler**
Discipler	**Discipler**	• Teach on sonship
• Listen for orientation of soul (acceptance, significance, security)	• Don't rescue	• Give spiritual direction in using spiritual practices to strengthen the reorientation
• Observe persona and be curious about the "inside of the cup"	• Ask penetrating questions	• Plan for obedience
• Are there "strivings"	• "What part of the Gospel don't you believe?"	• Reliance of the Spirit and hearing His voice
• Teach God's Word (challenging their orientation)	• Identify and break the shell protecting the soul (usually attachments related to acceptance, significance, and security)	
• Prayer for breaking the shell protecting the soul	• Gospel and God's perfections taught	
• Challenge disciple to live on mission	• Identify orphan spirit	

Physician of the soul

In this chapter, I will outline a simple model for equipping saints for soul work. It is not a program but rather a process of soul transformation with which we can engage one another. It could be integrated into any church program because it is a biblical approach to how soul transformation works. If we pull from all the previous chapters on understanding the three passions of the soul, a simple and reproducible model of training and disciple making could be established and implemented.

Imagine for a moment that all the saints in your church understood the three passions of the soul and were in community to engage one another daily about how their soul is being shaped by God's Spirit. Picture what would happen if your disciples were to become skilled and wise like an emergency room doctor who can diagnosis and treat whatever might come through the door on a Friday evening. A church filled with physicians of the soul would change the posture and character of the church in the world.

In many churches, if a person needs spiritual help, they must make an appointment with the pastor. Oftentimes the pastor performs triage and sends the patient to a counselor because they don't have time or the expertise to deal with deep soul issues. Actually, all our problems are deep soul issues! That is the work of discipleship! Please don't hear me say that counselors are not needed. What I am saying is that we are desperate for greater equipping of the saints in soul work because that is what is needed to make disciples who love God and others freely and fully.

Here is one model of equipping that could be used to equip saints in soul work. A diagram has been provided for reference as I walk through the process of soul discipleship in the rest of this chapter. It is not meant to be comprehensive but to lay out a simple and repeatable process that the saints can begin implementing in the context of any community of faith.

The model begins with listening to the orientation of the soul of the person. In an attitude of prayer and love for the person, the discipler anticipates the work of the Holy Spirit in ascertaining how the soul is oriented in regards to acceptance, significance, and security. Using all the senses that God has given us, we can observe the persona, the things being said, the tone, and attitude of the person. In this first movement of soul work, you are discovering what is beneath the surface. You can see behaviors (outside of the cup), but you are looking deeper into the soul. The orientation of the soul is revealed by being curious about what you see on the outside. What you are listening for are "inordinate attachments" (striving after things that are needed for peace and well-being). If you have SDI training, you will have an inside track and know where to look as SDI reveals our soul tendencies to seek identity and well-being.

This is not as difficult as you might think. People are always forming opinions about others by what they see. They watch a man directing his wife with forcefulness, and they think, *Wow! He seems so controlling!* But rather than stopping there, we need to ask the question, Why? Why does he feel the need to control his wife? What is going on in his soul? How is this behavior related to acceptance, significance, and security—the three ways love is expressed and the passions of the soul?

You observe another person in your small group, and you see that they are a workaholic. What is going on in their soul? Why do they work so hard and fail to care for their family? How is this related to the three passions of the soul? The striving after success while ignoring other needs in the family has its answers in the soul.

> *The biggest issue in the orientation phase is that people are not aware of what is going on in their own soul.*

The biggest issue in the orientation phase is that people are not aware of what is going on in their own soul. They may not even be aware of how their behavior is observed by others, let alone what is going on "inside the cup." Their greatest need is revelation. The orientation phase of soul work will require revelation. They need revelation that will move them to disorientation. If they don't get to disorientation, they will never reorient themselves around the Gospel and God's amazing love. Churches that allow people to stay oriented around anything other than the Gospel will never make disciples who will change the world.

God often initiates events in a person's life to reveal their orientation and move them into disorientation. Look what happened to Job. Moving from orientation to disorientation often involves pain. When we can no longer live in peace with the way our soul is oriented, we begin to seek other ways of addressing the deep need of our souls. As long as our soul is content with acceptance, significance, and security coming from man, we will not reorient our soul around the Gospel. It is when our husband leaves us, or our child gets cancer, or when we lose our job, or our best friend betrays us that we are willing to consider our soul's current orientation.

The Word of God is also powerful in challenging our orientation. The Scriptures are powerful and sharper than a two-edged sword. They speak into our lives, and the Holy Spirit challenges our soul. This is why the Word of God must be proclaimed, read, and meditated. God confronts our behavior and our soul, inviting us to a new way of living.

The role of the soul worker in this phase is to not only listen and discern the soul but to teach the Word. They are to live out a life that challenges the way others are orienting their lives. It is not just in the telling but in the living out of God's Word that revelation is made clear. I am always challenged afresh about my orientation of life when a person chooses to leave their home and serve in a third world country to bring the Gospel to a group of people with no access. The truth is incarnated before my eyes, and I can't ignore the challenge to my own soul.

Another way that orientation is revealed is when a church or Christ follower invites a person into mission for Christ. It is in the process of serving, especially if it requires dying to self in some way (financial, danger, incompetence, risk of rejection), that soul orientation is revealed. Ministries that allow people to stay comfortable miss the opportunity for moving people from orientation to disorientation.

Disorientation is the phase that is easiest to discern. This is when a person's life is in disarray. They are looking for new answers to questions they haven't asked before. The way they thought and behaved in the past is no longer adequate. They are searching. Depression, anger, panic, disillusionment, and discouragement are often expressions of disorientation—*God, why would you let this happen?*

When someone is in disorientation, we often want to rescue them from their pain. We want to find quick solutions to alleviate the agony. But in our rescuing, we may shortcut what God is doing. Remember the storm that Jesus prayed up while he sent the disciples right into the midst of it? He let them struggle at the oars before he revealed himself as the one who could still the storm. Often, if we are not desperate for changing our soul, we will put a Band-Aid on the cut and hope it will heal. I am not suggesting that we ignore the person and not help. What I am saying is that the help they need is not always a rescue rope but a push to explore their own soul for why they feel so unaccepted, insignificant, or unsafe. A skilled physician of the soul will take the opportunity to do soul surgery rather than fix the problem they are facing alone.

The physician of the soul will listen and ask penetrating questions, debrief what is going on inside of them. They will ask the key question, "What part of the Gospel don't you believe?" Ultimately, that is the issue that steals our peace and joy. We have built cisterns to hold water other than the Gospel of Christ, and they will never hold water. In this disorientation phase of soul work, that which is inside the soul is being revealed for what it is, and we are leading them to repentance.

It is in this phase that, in your attempt to go deeper into the soul, you may experience some resistance. The resistance may be passive or active. Passive resistance is unconscious. They may not even know they are being resistant. They simply can't go to the place you want to go. Our psychological defenses may keep us from opening up and letting someone in. Oftentimes, this is because of some deep pain. Active resistance is when a person is consciously aware of what is in their soul, but they are refusing to let you in. In either case, this resistance is the shell we referred to earlier that keeps the soul insulated from change. It must be broken. You cannot do soul work with the thick shell of protection intact. Ask God to break through the thick shell as you reflect the love of God to the person. They may need to know that you love them and you accept them, that they are significant to you, and that they are safe. As you reflect the love of God to them, you make the love of God tangible for them to grasp and to trust.

Before a person can move into the final phase of reorientation, there must be repentance. We have called this act of changing one's soul deep repentance because it isn't a matter of changing one's behavior alone but changing one's soul orientation. This crisis of disorientation is resolved by the Gospel. The Gospel teaches us that "God so loved...." His love expressed on the cross and the resurrection guarantees the work of redemption is complete and will be completed because it is His work. Our adoption as sons and daughters guarantees us that our acceptance cannot be taken away, that our significance doesn't need to be bolstered by anyone, and that our safety and security is certain. The crisis is averted when we yield to the Lover of our souls. We die to ourselves and cease striving for what only God can provide.

The soul physician will teach the attributes of God as, often, the person has either never known or forgotten that God is all-powerful, all-knowing, always present, perfect, sovereign, good, and merciful. In teaching of God's perfections, the person will grow in faith to trust God for the needs of his soul rather than himself or other men.

Once the person has turned his soul orientation from self to his Savior, he begins the phase of reorientation. Reorientation is all about growing in faith in trust that God's love is sufficient. If faith and trust are not present, the physician will need to go back and do more work. As faith and trust grow, the fear of man will decrease, and God will increase. Growing faith enables the person to live in obedience to the Gospel. The soul physician will explore what obedience to the Gospel looks like and helps the person to develop a plan forward. However, the issues of the soul are not left out of that plan. The soul must continue to be nurtured. The writing out of God's truth with regard to the three passions of the soul is helpful to remind the person of their identity. Spiritual habits that foster reflection on God's love and their identity will be needed for the soul to continue the journey of transformation.

This three phases of orientation, disorientation, and reorientation are repeated over and over again in the community of faith as we disciple one another's souls. The love of God is wide and deep and will take a lifetime to comprehend. But the results of this process should become evident as the fruit of the Spirit is released in our lives. The deep transformation of our souls will change our character and our behavior.

God invites us to be physicians of the soul. This simple three-phase process of discipleship could be replicated in the lives of Jesus's followers and be applied in any program and church structure. If we are truly going to make disciples who will change the world, we will need to apply ourselves to equipping all the saints. A thorough understanding of the soul and the Gospel is needed. What can you do to initiate a movement of soul discipleship in your context?

If the reader is interested in further training on being a physician of the soul, the author has developed extensive training which is available. You can review the options for different training opportunities at the following website: CHANGED2LEAD.ORG

Reflection Questions

1. Are you equipped to disciple someone's soul in the three phases of orientation, disorientation, and reorientation?

    If your answer is no, what kind of equipping would you need?

2. What would a vision of soul discipleship look like in your life and ministry? How can you begin?

3. What are the obstacles to seeing a movement of soul discipleship taking place in your life and ministry?

    How can you address those issues?

24

Implications for Discipleship

For if you love those who love you, what reward do you
have? Do not even the tax collectors do the same? And if
you greet only your brothers, what more are you doing than
others? Do not even the Gentiles do the same? You therefore
must be perfect, as your heavenly Father is perfect.

—Matthew 5:46–48

This book is not written as an attempt to lay out a new curriculum or program for discipleship. I have avoided that temptation and have sought simply to lay out some biblical foundations to discipleship that should be in any approach to discipleship. My hope was simply to challenge the church to think more deeply about what we are doing in the area of discipleship that would spur on greater conversation. Perhaps out of that conversation would come change that would deepen our commitment and effectiveness in making disciples who make disciples.

I have argued that the Gospel is a love story and love should be the guiding attribute of our Savior that should shape the making of disciples. Toward the end of the Sermon on the Mount, Jesus emphasizes that the character of his disciples is love. Why? Because that is the character of our Father. We are his children, and we are being transformed as his children to be like him. We were created to be image bearers of his love on earth: "You therefore must be perfect, as your heavenly Father is perfect" (Matt. 5:8). This love, which characterizes disciples of Christ, is different from the way the world loves. We are not to just love those who love us, but to love those who seek to hurt us and destroy us. That is a radical love! That is the love that Jesus demonstrated when he laid down his life for us. The word *perfect* (*telios* in Greek) has the idea of being complete, with nothing lacking.[48] The word *perfect* does not have a moral implication. Jesus is not speaking about moral perfectionism. He is not even saying that Christians must be better than other people. He is making it clear that the defining characteristic of Christians is their love that is distinct from the world. They don't just love those who love them but love people who can do nothing for them. In fact, they are to love those who are out to destroy them. Christians are to extend their arms like Christ did on the cross and embrace those who mock and spit on them.

There is a big difference between discipling people to live moral lives and teaching them to love like Christ. We can't settle for better law keepers. Churches that are filled with individuals who only love those who treat them well will stifle the cause of Christ in the world. How is that different from the world anyway? The church is too often filled with people who can tell you moral principles by which to live, but their souls are not driven by love. I am referring to a love for God and others. The need for self-worth is driving their behavior, and any hint of feeling attacked is worthy of a fight.

> **There is a big difference between discipling people to live moral lives and teaching them to love like Christ.**

I was with a pastor from Egypt recently who has a church of more than eight thousand disciples. He told me a story that illustrates the contrast between disciples who love God and disciples who love themselves. This church invested in raising up new churches and releasing the Gospel throughout Egypt and the entire Middle East. He told me about his recent visit to Syria which has been war-ravaged. The church in Syria has been largely destroyed by the extermination of Christians through ISIS. The church not only remains but is growing through the conversions of new Muslim believers. While preaching in one church in the evening, there was weeping and wailing that was heard outside the church. When they went outside to find out what was happening, they discovered hundreds of believers on their faces crying out to God in pain and mourning. That very night, ISIS had broken into several homes and kidnapped three members of their church and took them away.

This Egyptian pastor attempted to comfort these people by reminding them of God's power, presence, and protection as well as their eternal hope in Christ. However, it turned out that is not what the followers of Christ were mourning about. They were mourning that they themselves were not considered worthy of being taken for the cause of Christ and partake in the fellowship of Christ's suffering! Wow! These disciples loved God more than themselves. What a contrast to the typical believer in our church who is offended at a brother because he isn't chosen to lead the worship team or is unwilling to suffer the loss of friendship of a neighbor if they shared their love of Christ with them.

Perfect and complete love is what Christ came to live out. But that can only happen when we die to self. To die to self is to die to the need to advance oneself. Our motivation for acceptance, significance, and security through using others must die. That can only happen in us as we grow in our knowledge of God's love. He alone meets those needs and allows our selfishness to die and become powerless.

The Spirit of God is witnessing to our spirit that we are the sons of God. The more we understand our identity as sons and daughters, and the full extent of his love, the greater freedom we will have to love. The shackles of shame and selfishness are broken in the presence of a God who accepts us fully, provides and protect us, and desires intimacy with us because we are so significant to him. Our love grows as we understand our own sinfulness, and yet God continues to love. Like the woman who loved Christ greatly because she was a great sinner, so our love grows in light of his infinite grace and mercy which is powered by his extravagant love. Love is the only sufficient motivator of discipleship. Nothing else will do.

The church has experimented with discipleship through means other than growing in love for Christ. I include myself in those who have emphasized knowledge, holiness, and character with the hopes of making better disciples. In the end, we run out of motivation for living the kind of life that God requires—perfection. Not moral perfection, but a life motivated completely by love. Only love will drive my thirst for God's Word. Only love will drive me to obedience to God's law. Only love will change my character to be kind, gentle, patient.

We come to be a disciple through the Gospel of Christ, but it is also through the Gospel of Christ that we grow in our love. We make a mistake to think that the Gospel is simply an entrance into the life of Christ. It is also the way God transforms our souls. Once we understand that, the Gospel becomes central in all of discipleship. It drives our dying to self, the mission of God, and kingdom work. With this in mind, I propose the following six foci: growing self-awareness, training to be physicians of the soul, a community of faith, growth in the Father's love, Holy Spirit dependency, and spiritual habits.

Growing in Self-awareness

One day, I was having breakfast with someone who was sharing with me the drastic change that they had recently made in their life. He said that he never realized how angry and offensive he was toward others, and that God had revealed this to him. I was so pleased to hear this because I too have experienced his selfish and angry tone on more than one occasion. Just then, as he was finished sharing this new insight, the waitress came and put down his lunch on the table, including his coleslaw. As if something completely snapped in his brain, he jumped down her throat and said, "I ordered potato salad! Does that look like potato salad? Take it back." I was shocked. Hadn't he just realized what happened? I was glad that he had a revelation, but apparently, the revelation was incomplete! I took a risk and shared with him what I just experienced, watching him relate to the waitress. I will never forget the look on his face. He said, "What? Me? Really?" He was gracious and accepted my feedback, but it was a reminder of how little we really understand how we are perceived or what is going on inside our souls or the behavior that results.

Without self-awareness about what is going on inside our souls, how will we be able to address those issues? I don't know what I don't know? So how will I learn? I won't. Not unless someone helps me. The church must be engaged in the process of helping people become self-aware. Augustine and Calvin insisted that we cannot know God until we know ourselves. They are right.

Growing in self-awareness can be alarming and disconcerting. We tend to have defensive mechanisms that keep us from receiving feedback from others (shell of the soul). Oftentimes self-awareness initially brings pain and shame. We want to hide. But we must bring things out into the light.

It takes courage for a person to speak into someone else's life. To do so is to risk rejection, friendship, and even anger and attack. The church should be a place where self-awareness is developed because we truly love one another. We need to learn to risk. Speaking the truth in love can feel wrong. What business is it of mine anyway? Sometimes it is easier to simply avoid that person rather than confront or ask a question.

When I am speaking about self-awareness, I am not just talking about our persona—how we are perceived by others. I am also speaking about what is motivating our behavior. This will require greater skill and development on our part. The church is not in the practice of looking beneath the surface. The problem is at the root level, not just in the leaves. Discipleship will require a pursuit of the roots.

To die to myself, I must understand what is motivating my thoughts and behavior. Discipleship must go inside the cup and find out what mess is sticking and staining and stinking. We are passionate about ourselves. That will not die until we discover what we are holding onto, why, and who can release us from our own grip. This is more difficult than pointing out someone's failure to meet church expectations, or someone's weakness. Getting underneath what is happening requires a shovel, not a set of clippers.

Physician of the Soul Training

There are many times in Scripture when it records that "Jesus knew what was in their hearts" (Luke 9:47; Matt. 9:4). Jesus was not just concerned about people's behaviors, but he saw into their hearts. I don't think this is something that only the Son of God does. I believe that we must learn to discern what is going on inside the soul. We need to learn to be curious about the *why*. Otherwise, the comments Jesus made to the Pharisees about being only consumed about the outside of the cup rather than the inside makes little sense.

The first step in becoming a physician of the soul is to learn the anatomy of the soul. What drives the soul? What is the soul seeking? What does a soul's "shell" look like, and how is it developed and broken? If we don't understand the basic story of the Fall and the implications to the soul, we will not be able to address the soul and will remain focused on the outside of the cup.

Soul training cannot stop with simply learning the anatomy of the soul. We must also learn to hear the voice of the Spirit. No ministry takes place apart from the Spirit. He is the agent of sanctification and is the source of our spiritual gifts. We cannot change anyone. We are not called to do psychotherapy but to make disciples (I'm not pitting the two against one another but simply noting that not everyone is called to professional counseling). Disciple making is a spiritual endeavor that must be empowered by the Spirit of the living God.

Just as a doctor systematically goes through a routine when doing an exam to someone who is sick, we must have some fundamentals about what to look for in the soul and understand the symptoms. If the soul is seeking for acceptance, significance, and security apart from Christ, which one of these is driving the life of the disciple in front of me? How is this manifesting in their lives? Is there striving in their life? What can that tell me about what is going on in the soul?

We need to learn some skills in diagnosing, not only for others but also for ourselves. The practice of examining our own souls is biblical and necessary to soul development (1 Cor 11:28). Sometimes we need the help of others. Some have called this "spiritual direction." I prefer to simply call it discipling. There may be a place for those who are particularly skilled in giving spiritual direction, but we are all called to make disciples.

One time, I came home from a missions trip from a third-world country and found myself becoming extremely ill. My blood pressure and pulse would suddenly skyrocket and then fall. I would get nauseous and dizzy. It was so extreme that I went to the emergency room. As you know, most guys must be dragged to the hospital to see a doctor, but I was desperate. The doctor took my pulse and blood pressure. Nothing out of the ordinary. My temperature was fine. He said it was in my head and asked if I had previous panic attacks. Really? Just then, at that very moment, my pulse spiked and my pressure went off the charts, and I went to the ground. When I woke up, the doctor said I have a problem but that he had no clue what to do. He had never seen anything like that before.

At least he acknowledged there was a problem. By this time, I was beginning to think it was in my head. I called my missionary friend with much experience in a jungle hospital, and he said I should go to a hospital that services people from third-world countries. That made sense, but I asked him over the phone what he would do. He said he would take two medicines, as he was guessing that I had contracted a gastric parasite of some type. He e-mailed the prescription, and within a couple of days, I was healed.

Sometimes we need an expert. Not everyone will be able to deal with what is going on in our soul. God has gifted some to be used by him for this purpose. However, I do believe that those who are gifted should be training those of us who need to learn. Disciple makers need to be equipped to be physicians of the soul.

A Family Community

If the goal and motivation of discipleship is love, then a community of people are required to make disciples. You cannot love in a vacuum. We must learn to practice loving others like Christ loves us. Together we can learn how to love the world.

I use the word *family* because that is the metaphor that is most used in Scripture. We are the family of God (1 Pet. 2:17). We are children of God (1 John 3:10). My brothers and sisters make up this spiritual family (Matt. 12:49). We need each other! Fellowship is the family of God sharing in the same life of the Spirit. It was the practice of the church to gather together daily to encourage each other, be taught, pray, and break bread together.

If you consider the family unit and what happens in a family, you can understand the importance of the family in discipleship. The family structure was set up by God to be his instrument of growing infants into mature adults. This process requires members to work together in an atmosphere of openness and vulnerability. It is a place where we can be who we are and not be threatened because we are committed to each other. Families are not perfect and can get on our nerves. That is true of the family of God as well. However, we have one father and are united around him. We have one Savior who died for us all and loves us. We have one Spirit who dwells in us.

Neglecting the fellowship is to neglect God himself. To not love each other is to not love God. The fellowship is the laboratory of love in God's kingdom. It is the place where the soul can grow and mature. It is a confessional family as well. We are to confess our sins one to another (James 5:16) and not hide our sins. This is the place where our soul is made perfect.

The community of faith engages in relationships that understand the threefold process of orientation–disorientation–reorientation. The community interacts as a family of God on mission and experiences life together. It is in the context of life-changing experiences that we are shaped by the Spirit of God. Disciples need to be equipped to recognize and interact with other disciples about their orientation–disorientation–reorientation. One way this could happen is for them to learn the stories that impact the three passions of the soul (Ecclesiastes, Job, and Joseph). In the context of openness and vulnerability, the community helps the disciples process what is going on in their soul to help the reorient themselves around their identity in Christ.

Growing in Our Love for God

Perhaps it seems odd that in a book about discipleship, there is little that has been said about the spiritual disciplines. I have specifically not spoken about disciplines until now because I wanted to lay out the context for the disciplines. Disciplines apart from, or without the purpose of, growing in our love of God can simply be a means of achieving acceptance, significance, and security from God. In my experience as a pastor, the disciplines have often been a way for people to feel more loved by God. That is not their purpose. If used this way, they will not produce a "perfect" disciple but rather a "proud" disciple who believes they now deserve the love of God. If people fail to practice the disciplines as they believe, they will feel like a failure and feel unloved.

The disciplines (reading of the Word, prayer, fasting, confession, silence, meditation, journal, daily office, Sabbath, etc.) have the purpose for growing in our love for God. We can do all the disciplines for wrong reasons, which is why I have not brought them into the discussion. If they are used for the purpose of growing our souls to love with greater passion and love others with greater purpose, they are invaluable. But be careful, for our souls are quick to move into a religious spirit where we feel we deserve the blessing of God because of our practice of them.

I often struggle with the regular practice of spiritual disciplines for the very reason that I mention above. I have a habit of reading the Bible every year with a reading plan. This has been a regular habit that has enriched my soul. However, it has also been a source of pride and shame. Even though I know in my mind that my habit of reading God's Word or not reading God's Word does not impact my identity or standing with God, I find that when I am successful in reading (and journaling), I feel better about myself. I feel horrible about myself when I fall behind. Yes, I have a problem with a religious spirit. I have to remind myself that I read God's Word to grow in my love for him. If my failure to read creates in me a hunger for intimacy with God, then I know that I am on the right footing. The soul is deceptive and wicked. It is possible to do the disciplines and be feeding the flesh. No one was more successful than the Pharisees in living out the disciplines.

The disciplines are practices that nurture your soul in God's love. Your capacity to love is expanded, and your need to strive after love from others diminishes. We are set free to love others and serve them selflessly and sacrificially. If that is not happening, we are not using the disciplines in the manner in which they were intended.

Dependence on the Spirit

The ministry of discipleship cannot be accomplished in the flesh. Christ is our sanctifier. It is by the finished work of Christ that our sanctification is accomplished, and it is by the Spirit that lives are transformed. Romans 5:5 says, "And hope does not disappoint, because the love of God has been poured out in our hearts through the Holy Spirit who was given to us." Jesus Christ promised the sending of the Holy Spirit and to not leave us orphans (John 14:16–19). It is the Holy Spirit that pours out the love of God in our lives. Apart from the supernatural working of the Spirit in our souls, we will fail in the work of discipleship. This truth cannot be emphasized enough.

The Spirit of God is the one who does the discipleship and transformation. 2 Corinthians 3:18 declares, "And we all, with unveiled faces reflecting the glory of the Lord, are being transformed into the same image from one degree of glory to another, which is from the Lord, who is the Spirit." If we attempt to disciple without a full dependence on the Spirit of God, we will not be successful. No process, curriculum, teaching, or training can transform the soul. Soul transformation is a deep change that is intimately linked to a person's sonship "in Christ." The Spirit is the active agent in this deep change.

Discipleship ultimately requires a conscious and deliberate yielding of one's life to the Holy Spirit. A. B. Simpson taught that the more definite and thorough this act of surrender, the more complete and permanent will be the result. Discipleship is about yielding our lives in love to God and abandoning our need to search for love apart from him. Tozer said it like this, "He (Holy Spirit) wants to be Lord of your life. He wants to possess you so that you are no longer in command of the little vessel in the water you sail. You may be a passenger on board, or one of the crew, but you definitely are not in charge. Someone else is in command of the vessel." We can only yield our lives to God if we trust the love of God. The Holy Spirit is the one who transforms the soul by putting to death the flesh, which for a lifetime has pursued love apart from Christ.

These truths are not just theology and theory. They have practical application. The discipler must consciously be dependent on the Holy Spirit to do this deep, deep work. It will lead the discipler to be on their knees in prayer and be attentive to the voice of the Spirit. This is a spiritual ministry, and it must be done through the Spirit. Discipleship's goal is life controlled by the Spirit. We must be filled by the Spirit, allowing the indwelling Spirit of God to assume control over all areas of our lives (Eph 3:16–17).

Developing Spiritual Habits

So how do we know if we are making disciples of Christ? If our standard of measurement is the exercise of the disciplines, we might be misled. Doing the disciplines is not the goal of discipleship. They are only means. Those means can also be used to feed the flesh rather than the soul. How many people do you know who have spent their lives in the Word and have no love for people? Knowledge puffs up. It can nurture the flesh if it is done for the wrong reason.

Even the prayer life of a man is not an ideal standard of measurement. I have known people who pray constantly and with great passion, but their lives do not reflect a love for others. In fact, some use prayer as a means of getting the things they want for themselves. Often the failure of prayer to bring about their desires leads to disappointment, and ultimately, cynicism. Prayer can become a currency for the favor of God. They wrongly believe that prayer is primarily a way to have a better life. Prayer is meant for intimacy with God. It is the most personal way in which God connects with our soul. The temple curtain that divided the holy place from the holy of holies was rent in two by God himself. No priest is necessary for intercession, for we have direct access to the Father through Christ. God's Spirit is within us now, testifying that we are his sons and daughters. God uses prayer as a means of intimate communication between a Father and his children. Prayer, when properly understood and practiced, grows our intimacy with the very one who loves us most. We grow in our love because he loved us first (1 John 4:19).

The way we know that we have been successful in making disciples is that our disciples love God with all their heart, soul, mind, and strength and their neighbor as themselves. They love like Christ and live out loving obedience. They willingly serve others in love. They don't have to be prodded or coxed. They desire to spend time with God and enjoy his intimacy. They demonstrate a heart for lost people and rearrange their priorities to bring the good news to those who have never heard it. They talk about their good, good Father all the time. They live in peace with others as far as it is possible because they don't strive to have their own way, yielding to other's preferences and needs.

Perhaps we need to change our matrix for measuring a fully formed disciple so that we will focus on the right things. For sure, it is more difficult to measure a loving soul than to measure how many people come to church on a Sunday or, say, pray twenty minutes a day, but I believe that if we start with a different goal, we will end up in a different place. I pray that we make disciples who are growing in their knowledge of the love of God. According to Paul, we can never exhaust the height and depth, width and breath of his infinite love (Eph 3:17–19). But that should be our prayer for our disciples, as it was for Paul.

The most famous quote of Martin Luther, which came from a partial fragment that he wrote while hiding from the church in a castle, was "Love God and sin boldly." The context of this quote was that Luther was writing to Melanchthon about whether or not to continue the practices of the church that were unclear as to their sinfulness. He was not for sin to abound, nor was he against holiness. Although some have taken his words to give a license for sin because God's infinite grace will abound all the more, I don't think that is what he had in mind. His whole point was that if you give your life to love God, you don't have to fret about your sin. Yes, you will sin. That is a given. But you will be in a good place if you focus your attention on loving God. Luther was right. His advice is good for us today as well.

If the discipler will give themselves to the above foci, I believe we will see a growth in our disciples, which otherwise we might not see. These are only principles to guide our thinking, based on the Scriptural emphasis and specifically the teaching of Christ. I find it fascinating that Jesus did not give us curriculum to make disciples. He gave us himself. And he gave us the Spirit.

APPENDIX

SDI Triangle and Descriptors of Seven MVS

The soul has three needs: acceptance, significance, and security. We all have these three needs, but we are wired to achieve self-worth differently depending on where we are on the SDI triangle. Learning our MVS (Motivational Value System) gives us insight in how we seek love apart from God. It also helps us to understand why we behave like we do.

The SDI inventory will pinpoint your dot on the triangle to display the mixture of your motivations and what is most important to you. You can also read the descriptors and identify with the one that is most like you.

Focus of attention for each MVS Region

ACCEPTANCE (SOUL NEED)

Blue: Altruistic-Nurturing/People

People who are motivated by the protection, growth, and welfare of others. They have a strong desire to help others who can genuinely benefit.

- Try never to be a burden to others, preferring to give help rather than receive it.
- Be open and responsive to the needs of others.
- Defend the rights of others with courage and conviction, sometimes without claiming their own rights in the process.

Conflict Triggers for Blue

- Relationships are not regularly maintained.
- People are selfish or unconcerned about others.
- Display of emotion is disregarded, ignored, or punished.

SIGNIFICANCE (SOUL NEED)

Red: Assertive-Directing/Performance

People who are motived by task accomplishment and achieving results. They have a strong desire to set goals, take decisive actions, and claim earned rewards.

- Challenge the opposition, actively engaging to overcome resistance.
- Take quick action, seeking immediate results.
- Compete for authority, responsibility, and positions of leadership.

Conflict Triggers for Red

- Pursuit of desired goal is lost through unnecessary, time-consuming collaboration or emotional considerations.
- People appear gullible, indecisive, or incapable of action.
- The desire to get an immediate outcome is viewed as irrational and uncaring.

SECURITY (SOUL NEED)

Green: Analytic-Autonomizing/Process

People who are motivated by meaningful order and thinking things through. They have a strong desire to pursue independent interests, to be practical, and to be fair.

- Be cautious and thorough, documenting details to ensure accuracy.
- Be objective and logical, practically thinking things through before taking action.
- Manage their emotions, diminishing the impact of feelings on outcomes, and relying on logical interaction as the primary communication style.

Conflict Triggers for Green

- They are forced to do things someone else's way without adequate explanation.
- They think that others do not take things seriously, lose focus, or trivialize the importance of a calm, orderly world in which to live and work.
- The opposition or conflict is based on emotion.

SIGNIFICANCE AND ACCEPTANCE (SOUL NEED)

Red-Blue: Assertive-Nurturing/Performance and People

People who are motivated by the maximum growth and development of others. They have a strong desire to direct, persuade, or lead others for the benefit of others.

- Persuade and energize others, often resulting in the growth and development of others.
- Be positive, enthusiastic, and forward-thinking.
- Recognize the importance of results and the needs of others.

Conflict Triggers for Red-Blue

- The guidance they offer is not accepted but instead challenged or even rejected.
- Other people are negative about options and possibilities, refusing to get involved.
- Plans that could lead to others' success are overruled, and the human cost of decisions is ignored.

SIGNIFICANCE AND SECURITY (SOUL NEED)

Red-Green: Judicious-Competing/Performance and Security

People who are motivated by intelligent assertiveness and fairness in competition. They have a strong desire to develop strategy and assess risks and opportunities.

- Challenge opposition through thoughtful process and strategy.
- Defend logical positions with energy and forcefulness.
- Provide rational leadership that can assess risks and opportunities.

Conflict Triggers for Red-Green

- Others behaving in an impulsive or emotional way.
- They are being forced to operate within the constraints of rules that are illogical or counterproductive.
- Others perceive their choices as mindless or aggressive.

ACCEPTANCE AND SECURITY (SOUL NEED)

Blue-Green: Cautious-Supporting/Acceptance and Security

People who are motivated by developing self-sufficiency in self and others and to help others help themselves.

- Be patient, soft-spoken, and conscientious when relating with others.
- Be fair, logical, and principled in the consideration of other people's needs.
- Want to be included in decisions about matters affecting the welfare of others.

Conflict Triggers for Blue-Green

- Solutions are being dictated, and power is being used to force outcomes.
- They are being pushed to move ahead before they are ready.
- Clarification of issues and emotions is blocked, forcing action without reflective discussion.

SIGNIFICANCE-SECURITY-SIGNIFICANCE (EQUAL NEED)

Hub: Flexible-Cohering/People-Performance-Process Equal

People who are motivated by flexibility and adapting to others or other situations. They have a strong desire to collaborate with others and to remain open to different options.

- Experiment with different ways of behaving.
- Be flexible, social, playful, and collaborative.
- Examine the situation from multiple perspectives.

Conflict Triggers for Hub

- Others are excluded from the group or treated indifferently.
- They can see that several mutually exclusive opportunities have equal value, and it is not clear that any one of them is better than the others.
- Others restrict their ability to change, insisting on only one approach or solution.

Concepts of the SDI are printed with permission. The concepts of the soul printed in all caps are that of the author, not of the SDI.

soul

Pre-release free shipping

$0.00

Additional Information

How did you find us?:
FaceBook
Are you a certified Changed2lead/SDI faciliator?:
Yes

https://changed2lead.com

Changed2lead LLC • 13 Burt Ave., Pompton Plains, NJ 07444, USA

Order Invoice

Order Number: **00013** (placed on March 31, 2017 11:46AM EDT)

BILLED TO:
Peter Pendell
29 Roberts Circle
BASKING RIDGE, NJ, 07920
United States
CC: XXXX-3476
plpendell@gmai.com

SHIPPING TO:
Peter Pendell
29 Roberts Circle
BASKING RIDGE, NJ, 07920
United States
908-881-9497
US MAIL DELIVERY

Order Summary

ITEM	QTY	UNIT PRICE	SUBTOTAL
Three Passions of the Soul SQ0671696	1	$15.99	$15.99

Item Subtotal		$15.99
Shipping & Handling		$0.00
Discount Savings		- $0.00
Tax		$0.00
TOTAL		**$15.99**

Discounts

ENDNOTES

1 David J. Kennedy, *Plant a Seed...and Watch It Grow!* (Ft. Lauderdale, FL: Evangelism Explosion III International, 1983).

2 C. S. Lewis, *The Screwtape Letters: With Screwtape Proposes a Toast* (San Francisco: Harper San Francisco, 2001), 12.

3 Martyn Lloyd Jones, "The Moral Attributes of God," *Great Doctrines of the Bible* (Wheaton, IL: Crossway Books, 2003), 78.

4 Ibid, 74.

5 Andrew Murry, *Humility* (Minneapolis, MN: Bethany House, 2001), 17.

6 "Evangelical Catholic Apologetics." Retrieved October 7, 2015, www.biblicalcatholic.com/apologetics/s20.htm.

7 "The Ten Commandments." Retrieved March 3, 2016, www.the-ten-commandments.org.

8 Cornelius Plantinga Jr., *Not the Way It's Supposed to Be: A Breviary of Sin?* (Grand Rapids: B. W. Eerdmans, 1995).

9 Daniel Delzell, *The Christian Post*, retrieved February 25, 2015.

10 Paul David Tripp, Timothy S. Lane, and David Powlison, *How People Change Study Guide: How Christ Changes Us by His Grace* (Greensboro, NC: New Growth Press, 2010).

11 Larry Crabb, "Spiritual Direction" (a presentation in Colorado Springs, CO, June 1, 2015).

12 S. Tompkins, "Bernard of Clairvaux on Love", Christian History Institute, https://www.christianhistoryinstitute.org/study/module/bernard/.

13 "On Loving God", accessed January 2, 2016, www.ccel.org/node/84

14 K. Benjamin, "5 Shocking Ways We overestimate Ourselves", *Cracked Magazine*, May 2015.

15 H. R. Segelken, "Americans are not as nice as they think they are", *Cornell Chronicle*, March 2014, accessed December 8, 2015 from http://www.news.cornell.edu/search/site/Epley.

16 Segelken, "Americans are not as nice as they think they are"

17 *Merriam-Webster, Inc. Merriam-Webster's collegiate dictionary*. Springfield, MA, 2003.

18 Augustine, & H. Chadwick, *Confessions*, 29, 1991.

19 John Calvin & Wood, B. R., *Biblical Christianity: An easier-to-read and abridged version of the classic "Institutes of the Christian Religion" by John Calvin first published in 1536*, 1982, 17.

20 Calvin and Wood, *Biblical Christianity*, 19.

21 Calvin and Wood, *Biblical Christianity*, 25.

22 G. L. Sittser,. *Water from a deep well: Christian spirituality from early martyrs to modern missionaries*, (Downers Grove: InterVarsity Press, 2007), 282.

23 Sittser, *Water from a deep well*, 282.

24 G. Kittel, In *Theological dictionary of the New Testament: Volume 6*, (Grand Rapids, MI: Eerdmans Publishing, 1964),367.

25 M. Tenney (Ed.), *The Zondervan Encyclopedia of the Bible: Volume 4*, (Grand Rapids, MI: Zondervan, 1975), p. 278.

26 Nelson Mendela, "Acceptance speech of the President Nelson Mandela, at the Nobel Peace Prize Award Ceremony," accessed February 12, 2106 http://www.anc.org.za/show.php?id=4114.

27 Tim Scudder, *Working with SDI (2nd ed.)*, (Carlsbad, CA: Personal Strengths Publishing, 2014), 7.

28 Scudder, *Working with SDI*.

29 Kittel, *The Theological Dictionary of the New Testament; Volume 5*, 367.

30 Christine Comaford, "Three Things all Human Beings Crave," *Forbes*, March 2013, 35.

31 Robert Rohr and A. Ebert and P. Heinegg, *The Enneagram: A Christian Perspective*, (St. Louis, MS: The Crossroad Publishing Company, 2001), 26.

32 Don R. Riso, and Russ Hudson, *The wisdom of the enneagram: The complete guide to psychological and spiritual growth for the nine personality types*, (St. Louis, MS: The Crossroad Publishing Company, 1999).

33 Renee Roserio, (2012, June 6). "Motivations and the Enneagram," *Psychology Today*, June 6 2012, accessed December 12, 2015 www.enneasight.com.

34 David K. Naugle, "St. Augustine's Concept of the Disordered Love and its Contemporary Application, Southwest Commission on Religious Studies," *Theology and Philosophy of Religion Group*, March 12, 1993.

35 Morris Dirks, *Forming the leader's soul: An invitation to spiritual direction*, (Soul Formation, 2013), 67.

36 Ignatius, D. L. Fleming, *The spiritual exercises of St. Ignatius: A literal translation and a contemporary reading.* (Boston MA: Institute of Jesuit Resources, 1978).

37 Peter Scazzero, *The emotionally healthy leader: How transforming your inner life will deeply transform your church, team, and the world* (Grand Rapids MI: Zondervan, 2015), 55.

38 Ebert Rohr, R. *The Enneagram: A Christian Perspective*, 278.

39 Paul D. Tripp, *Awe: Why it matters in everything we think, say, or do.* (Wheaton IL: Crossway, 2015).

40 Aiden W. Tozer, *The Root of righteousness* (Camp Hill, PA: Wingspread Publishers, 1955), 36.

41 Jack Frost, *Spiritual slavery to spiritual sonship,* (Shippensburg PA: Destiny Image Publishers, 2006), 56.

42 Walter Brueggemann, *The message of the Psalms: A theological commentary,* (Minneapolis MN: Augsburg Press, 1984).

43 Kittel, *The Theological Dictionary of the New Testament; Volume 4,* 1098.

44 Alexander B. Bruce, *Training of the twelve.* (Grand Rapids MI: Kregel Publishing, 1988).

45 *"Quotations of G.K. Chesterton,"* accessed April 20, 2016 http://www.chesterton.org/quotations-of-g-k-chesterton.

46 Lauren Suval, "The Relationship Between Happiness and Gratitude," *World of Psychology August 9, 2012,* accessed April 22, 2016 http://psychcentral.com/blog/archives/2012/08/09/the-relationship-between-happiness-and-gratitude.

47 Richard Stearns, *The hole in our gospel: The answer that changed my life and might just change the world* (Nashville, TN: Thomas Nelson Publishers, 2009).

48 Kittel, *The Theological Dictionary of the New Testament; Volume 8,* 1157.

NOTES

NOTES

NOTES

NOTES

p.79 Mandella: Set free vs. Living free
p.164 Brueggemann: orientation → disorientation →
                                reorientation

changed2lead.org